David Hernandez graduated in May 2017 from Argo Community High School in Summit, Illinois, which is situated very near Midway Airport on the southwest side of Chicago and is currently a freshman at the University of Illinois at Chicago (UIC).

In my twenty five years of being a public school educator I have met very few young adults like David Hernandez. His zest for life, thirst for learning, and passion for sharing his life lessons with others are to be admired. Through these stories and words of wisdom you will be encouraged to challenge your own thinking, consider how you look at life's many and varied situations, and manage your daily challenges and successes.

Thank you David Hernandez for having a tremendous impact on my life and for encouraging me to Never Give Up in helping young adults reach their full potential.

- JILL KINGSFIELD
Argo Community High School Superintendent (District 217)

PROLOGUE : WHY NOT?

When I was a kid my mom would give my brother and I the same lectures over and over again after dinner. I practically memorized them. They were always about respecting others, working hard, being grateful and not doing stupid things because you could get in trouble. Because I was hearing these lectures as a child, they became more and more natural to comprehend. I would say "Duh', of course it doesn't make sense to be mean because that's not nice." That's what my 8-year-old self would think. However, It was in the 6th grade when I first started seeing in front of me what my mom would talk about. I saw the precautions and opportunities my mother had predicted. I was practically connecting the dots throughout middle school and unconsciously following the guide my mom had taught me. Even through some bumps in the road, I graduated middle school feeling pretty good and happy with who I was. Some of my classmates had no idea what they were doing and struggled to make sense out of their existence and be happy with who they were. I'm not saying every middle school kid should know those things by the time they graduate, but If I had a pretty good idea of who I was, why couldn't they?

I then remembered my mom walking me to school throughout all of my elementary years even though the school was practically in our backyard. I remember my mom telling me "I'd rather have you bring friends over to the house than you going over to theirs." I remember my mom making sure I always had on clean clothes or something to drink when it was hot. I remember my mom telling me to call my grandma to ask her how she was doing because she liked attention. I remember my mom telling me to always be there and help my older brother who had Spina Bifida (a birth condition where the spinal cord fails to develop properly). I remember my mom telling me to be organized with the stuff in my room. I remember my mom telling me to never buy anything that I didn't need. I remember my mom reminding me of the value of education since she never had any. I realized that for every lecture my mother gave me, there was someone in the world who *didn't* receive it. My father preferred to work double and have my mom stay home to take care of my brother and I than to have both of them working. I didn't have the biggest house, fanciest car, or the most toys, but I had a mother who loved me dearly and taught me how to be human. She taught me valuable lessons that I realized most adults around me didn't know.

I used to think that being intelligent correlated with getting older. I used to think that people like Michelangelo, Shakespeare, Picasso, Einstein and John Lenon were out-of-this-world geniuses that were probably born with some amazing talent or super scientific genes. Since these legendary figures were also older than I was, I thought that every adult in the world was mature and very smart. Boy, was I wrong. As I got older and older I felt wiser and wiser. I remember being at a kid's birthday party talking to a group of six mothers on how to be a good parent. I was ten at the time. The women would laugh and tell me that they weren't laughing at me, but laughing at the fact that a little boy was saying some of the truest things about parenthood. All I was really doing was repeating what my mom taught me.

I couldn't help but notice the negative and unhappy people around me as I got older, too. The thought I had about everybody being mature once they got older was proven very wrong. I'm not saying I was some sort of saint growing up, for I have made many mistakes of my own. But even with the severity of my mistakes, I've been able to learn from them and share the moral of my story today, while I've seen others who took the wrong route and are too embarrassed to tell their story. I also thought that one needed to live through an entire lifetime to write a book about how to live life. I thought one needed to be old and grey like Mr. Feeny or Master Shifu to give advice. But after surviving high school for four years and being able to sacrifice and accomplish many things, I figured, *why not*?

My high school experience ended up being one about making a name for myself and creating opportunities. I was the kid who was barely passing his classes but was involved in everything that had to do with his passion. I was the kid who created events in the library to let others kids express themselves with their talents. I was the kid who was willing to put on the mascot suit to bring joy and energy. I was the kid who made Speech Team look cool. I was the kid who fell in love with his hobby and decided that that's what he wanted to do for the rest of his life.

Throughout high school I learned some of the most valuable things that could change one's life. I learned the art of not being whack, loving myself, forgiving myself, being grateful, acting and reacting, doing it myself, living minimally, not giving up, finding my escape, finding my passion, understanding people, being a leader, being free, and not procrastinating, all through the help of self-reflection and the relationships I built with mentors, family, and friends.

Over time I've noticed that people who are familiar with and practice these concepts are the "geniuses" of our time. We live in a time period where negativity is inevitable. It's everywhere you go. It's in your social media, your news, your city, community, home, hallways, anywhere you can think of. Being positive today is the new abnormal. People don't understand happiness anymore. The people that understand the art and practice of positivity are those who live a life full of happiness while others stare in jealousy. Positive people are the modern day Picasso's, Michelangelo's, Shakespeare's, Einstein's and Lenon's. They see life through a different perspective that creates happiness, rather than waits for it. A perspective that appreciates, rather than complains. A perspective that moves forward, rather than going nowhere. I was able to learn all these concepts with 15% of it coming from mentors, 10% coming from sources, and 75% from personal experiences. I also learned all of them in high school, back when I was a little munchkin with a dream.

Over the years I've dedicated myself not only to my passion, but to helping spread positivity throughout my community. I've been teaching poetry and dance classes to students since I was a Freshman. I've been mentoring since I was a Junior. The moment I would learn something new, I'd share it with the youth around me. Children are truly the only hope we have in this world. If we do not nurture them correctly, history will only repeat. We must teach the youth to be the change in history, not the consequence of it.

I decided to put together everything I've learned so far and write a book. Earlier this year I presented the book in 15-minute lectures to my very first Munchkin who is her Senior year of high school. Later, I presented the 16 chapters to a Facebook group of 30 students called, you guessed it, "David's Munchkins." This book is specifically dedicated to high school kids to learn some valuable lessons that might not be taught in the classroom and could ultimately change their life. I was blessed enough to learn and apply these concepts to my life and witness the great benefits that come from it. I know, it sounds crazy coming from someone who literally just graduated high school a couple of months ago. Even then, I will proudly say that I don't know everything, but I do know some things. So with that being said: Ladies and gentleman, here in its grand debut, I present to you: *The Munchkin Guide*.

To Heidi Soria & Natalie Cross.

My First Munchkins.

CHAPTER 1 : DON'T BE WHACK

Two years ago I was at a Slam Poetry camp at UIC College hosted by an organization called "Young Chicago Authors", which is a cool program that dedicates themselves to community work through Poetry all throughout the city of Chicago. The leader of the organization is an amazing teacher named Kevin Coval, who is also a legendary poet. One day someone asked him what was his number one key to success. I'll never forget the way he replied. All he said was "Don't Be Whack." The phrase "Don't Be Whack" means three things: *Don't Be Afraid To Learn & Be Adventurous*, *Don't Be Afraid To Be Yourself* and *Remember Your Limits*.

Don't Be Afraid To Learn & Be Adventurous

I know a lot of people who say "I don't like Chinese food", but when you ask them if they've ever tried it, they say "No." How can you like or dislike something if you've never tried it? How can you be good at anything if you've never practiced it? Two years ago marks the very first time I went roller skating. I had never done it before, so I fell a lot, and I mean *a lot*. But at the end of the night I didn't say I sucked at roller skating, I just said I needed to practice it more. You're not necessarily bad at something the first moment you try it. Nowadays, if someone tries a new sport, activity or skill and it doesn't go so well, they think "It's destiny. I'm awful and I'll never do it again." No! Don't do that!

Everything in life takes practice. Sometimes you'll try a new thing and you might not be great at it, but you'll love it so much that you'll want to get better at it. Two years ago I was playing competitive Badminton for the first time. I was terrible at it, but I loved it so much! I practiced and practiced and eventually became a pretty good player. Simple as that! Don't be afraid to practice something new! As you try new things, you'll also learn more about yourself. Not being whack will lead you to the decision of going sky-diving. However, let's say sky-diving ended up being really terrifying for you and you pooped yourself mid-air. Chances are you'll never go sky-diving again. If you decided not to be whack and tried new food but got a terrible stomach ache, you probably won't want to eat that food ever again either. But now, at least you've had those experiences to firmly say you'll never do them again, instead of pondering over what the experience would've been like.

Not being whack is not only about trying new things, it's about *learning* new things as well! Search up random information! Learn about the history of your favorite music genre. Read a new book. Watch a new movie. Look up behind-the-scenes videos. Look up different cultures from different ethnicities. Learn a new language. Learn! Learn! Learn! If all you know is what you know, what you do, what you eat, and your favorite TV show, you're being whack! You never know what you'll discover. I used to think that Theatre was so corny and that I would never try it. However, I knew by my Sophomore year that I wanted to be a performer of some sort. I could've been whack and said "No, Theater isn't for me. I'm going to stick to rapping or something else", and never have taken the opportunity. But instead I said "I'm not going to be whack. I can't sing, but whatever, I'll audition for the school musical anyway." Theatre is now the number one thing I want to do for the rest of my life. All because I decided to try something new. I wasn't good at it, but I was willing to practice and work hard to be decent. I loved it that much.

Don't Be Afraid To Be Yourself

In my last year of high school, I volunteered to be the mascot. To be honest with you, I could've quit the moment I realized our sport teams weren't so great. I could've quit when I realized we had the whackest student body on the planet. But I didn't. I did not let that stop me from being who I am: The cheery, outgoing person who dances with no music and sings out loud. I was just being myself. I had people telling me that I was their favorite part of the game, but I also had people telling me to shut up when I was trying to cheer. Regardless of what the reaction was, I didn't care. I chose to never take their opinions seriously. When it came to other people's opinions I always asked myself three things:

1) *Do they know me?*
2) *Do they care about me?*
3) *Have they done anything for me?*

If the answer was "NO" to all three, I could've cared less what they thought about me! I refused to be whack because of the opinions of other people. I remember going to study hall rooms promoting events that were taking place in the school's library and seeing people put their heads back down the moment they heard my voice. I would call them out for being whack right before I left the room instead of leaving with the sense of defeat. People prevent themselves from enjoying life because of opinions of complete strangers. Have you ever met someone who was shy, but completely outgoing once you got to know them? People call it "breaking their shell" but that wouldn't be necessary if they would've just been themselves in the first place. I've tried making new friends and had the result of people wanting nothing to do with me, and people who ended up being my best friends. Regardless of how anything goes, I can say I tried it, succeeded or failed instead of being bored in silence or pondering with the question of "What if?"

Also, don't be afraid to be wrong! If I confidently answered "2+2=5" and the whole class looked at me in a weird way, I wouldn't restrain myself from answering any other question for the rest of the year. I would simply say "Am I wrong? If I am, educate me and tell me what's the right answer." If you are never wrong, you'll never know what's right! Nowadays we treat being wrong as a punishment. If I told someone I've never read a Harry Potter book, they might look at me like I'm crazy, the same I would look at someone if they told me they don't know who the Ninja Turtles were! It's okay to not know and be wrong, as long as you're willing to learn and understand what's right or what's new.

Remember Your Limits

If someone tells me "Let's go to a party!", I'll say "Bet!" If someone asks me to try new food? Bet! Go on a Roller Coaster? Bet! But if someone offered me to jump off a cliff, do drugs, or drink alcohol, I would say "...Nah', I'm okay." I'm not being whack, I'm just thinking about three things:

1) My Safety
2) My Morality
3) The Consequences

Reading a new book is practically harmless, but trying a new food could lead to a bad stomach ache. Every new thing you experience has its own good and bad. I chose jumping off a cliff, doing drugs and drinking because those are my extremes. I, personally, reject those things because I don't feel safe, they don't align with my morality, and I know there are severe consequences that come with it. That's just me. There are people who might think the opposite, which I hope none of them are you. When I say don't be whack, I'm not saying to be a "Yes-Person" and accept everything. Not being whack is about you recognizing an appropriate opportunity to try and learn a new thing. Every person will have their limits and boundaries. I'm usually down for whatever, but if you told me to pet some goats and feed them, I will probably say no, because I'm afraid of animals (Seagulls chasing me when I was little traumatized me. It's okay, you can laugh.) and I don't feel safe. One day I went to the Zoo with my girlfriend. Although it was really fun, I was terrified most of the time. That's just me. I know people who have been traumatized by a roller coaster and won't get on one ever again. You're not being whack, you're just being yourself and knowing what to try and what not to. That's perfectly okay, as long as you've had the experience or enough perception to form an opinion.

At the end of the day, don't be afraid to try and learn new things! You'll never know what you'll love or hate! Always, however, keep in mind your safety, your morality and the consequences! Live life, it doesn't last that long!

Chapter Challenge!

Write down 5 things you want to try/learn this season!

This can be wanting to make new friends, a movie you've been wanting to watch, restaurants you want to try, cultures you want to learn about, places you want to go, something new!

CHAPTER 2 : PASSION

Finding your passion is hard and easy. It's easy to find, but hard to accept, or vice versa. Passion, at least in the definition I use, is loving something unconditionally through its ups and downs. I usually think of the color red. Something beautiful. Something you want to hold on for the rest of your life. Passion could be towards a person, an object, an activity, ect. However, if you don't know what your passion is yet, that's completely okay. If you don't know, please refer to Chapter One! If you do have some idea of what you're passionate about, this is for you. Passion comes with two things: *A Change in Time & Perception,* and *Spiritual Fulfillment.*

A Change in Time & Perception

I wasn't a big fan of school. Some of my classes bored me to death. I would look at the clock that would read 12:40. Five minutes later I would look at it again and it would read 12:35. I couldn't believe my eyes. It's like I was going to be trapped in there forever. However, there are also moments when I was doing something I liked or was with people I like where I couldn't tell if 15 minutes or 4 hours had passed. That just shows to prove that time literally changes depending on what we like and don't like to do. When you're deeply involved in your passion, when you're in the zone, in your element, time tends to go by faster. I used to go to after school

Theatre practice and be shocked when it was time to go home at six. I was ready to keep working for another three hours. When I was playing Badminton I couldn't tell if I had been playing for 30 minutes or two hours. But when I was in math class, time was clearly going backwards. One of the easiest ways to find your passion is by recognizing how fast time flies when you're doing a certain thing. Some of you might realize you really like cooking, drawing, reading books, organizing files, or playing an instrument by noticing how invested you're in it to the point where hours pass by swiftly.

Passion also comes with unconditional love: loving through the good, the bad and the ugly. I remember being very passionate about basketball until my Freshman year. I had played two years in middle school and worked hard to become a good player. However, once I got to high school, the competitive level got to be a bit too much for me. I loved the sport, but I was not willing to go through the motions and adapt to high school basketball. I loved it, but I wasn't passionate about it. You'll start to see that for yourselves. There will be a lot of things you love, but won't necessarily die for. You might love running, but you won't get up at 6AM every day to jog a mile. You might love acting, but can't stand when a director tells you what to do. That's perfectly fine. It's okay to love things, but when you're passionate about something, you go through the ups and downs. If you're passionate about cooking, you'll have to go through the countless recipes you'll mess up. If you're passionate about modeling, you're going to have to face the strict diets. If you're passionate about being a mascot, you have to get used to that really hot suit. When it was the week of a show for Theatre, I would have really bad back pains after every show. However, I would've done the show every night for two months if I could! At the end of the day, we're all slaves to something. If we're doing something we don't like, we call it slavery. If we're doing something we love, we call it "doing whatever it takes." Passion changes time and perception.

Spiritual Fulfillment

What I'm about to say next might contradict everything you've ever learned in life. First and foremost, *Prioritize Your Passion.* Do what makes you happy at least for an hour a day, or even just for 15 minutes. Do it. In life we're taught to do what you have to do first, and then "play." Work now and then play later. Do your schoolwork and then go outside. Go to work and then go out with your friends. Go work your 9-to-5 and then go to the club. Forget that. Prioritize your passion. In school I was never a great student because I loved music and art too much. I was involved in Band, Speech Team, Choir, Theatre, Teaching Poetry, Creating Open-Mic Events, being a Mascot, anything I could get my hands on. But because of my progress report-card every semester, there would always be a huge fight at my house with my parents because I would be borderline failing classes. That's because when I would get home from school I would work on my passion, hence, time flying and it being 11PM without doing any of my homework. This by no means is a suggestion to be me. PLEASE DON'T BE ME. It was a tough game to play (but I did it and graduated with Honors too). The point I'm trying to make is that I was very successful within the activities I participated in because I prioritized my passions. You shouldn't go the extreme level I did, but always keep your passion alive somehow. The other option doesn't go to well. Check this.

I know a person who graduated with me that loved art just as much as I did. They loved writing. They wrote plays, stories and poetry, but they went a different route. They chose to work now and play later. However, they had such a heavy work load that they never got a chance to play. This person, by Senior year, had all AP classes. They had tons of homework and were tired by the time they were done. They went to sleep, woke up and did it all over again. This person told me that the only thing they regretted in their high school career was not prioritizing their passion. They said that the school work literally drained the creativity out of them. With that being said, don't do the same thing! Find a way to prioritize your passion! By making time for your passion, whether it's only 15 minutes a day, it keeps it alive within you. Yes, you will have to do plenty of things in your life that you will not like to do. Taking all AP classes will definitely help you in the long run, but it will come with some heavy work and some sacrifices. If you keep your passion close to you, you will always have something to look forward to and be happy with! That's what I did. Did I sacrifice some academics? Unfortunately. Was it worth it?

Every bit of it. Do I recommend it? NO! What I do recommend is always keeping your passion an arms-length away.

As you get older and start making bigger decisions, keep this in mind: *Money Doesn't Buy Happiness. It really doesn't.* I currently work at a Texas Roadhouse Restaurant as their mascot, Andy The Armadillo. I love my job so much, while there are many others who don't. One day I was in the back putting my costume away next to a guy smoking a cigarette. He was clearly very tired. He said he had started working about eight hours before I came in. He told me he works 55 hours a week and only has one day off. I asked him what he does with all that money he gets. He told me he wakes up, goes to pay his bills, goes to work, goes home, sleeps, wakes up, and does it all over again. He left me with one sentence: "Being an adult sucks." One of the waitresses I know makes almost a $100 a day. One day she even made $250. But there's not a single day where she doesn't complain about how much she hates her job. There are millionaires in the world who hate their jobs and their lives. They focus on the benefits of what they're doing rather than the joy of doing what they do. They don't have a passion. They think money is the passion, but it's not. There's many people who would rather make less and be happy than make more and be miserable. There's a lot of rich people who only use money to buy fake materialistic things to portray as fake happiness. Two years ago I worked with a Chicago artist name Chai Tulani. He talked about doing a show and opening up for a rapper named Jay Electronica (Who's a big name in the Hip Hop world). I was like "Woah! That's amazing! How much did you make?" and he said he only made $11 that night. I looked at him with a shocked face. "Only $11?" He looked at me dead in the eye and said "I would do it all over again. I loved it so much. I had the time of my life. I was spiritually fulfilled." My mind was blown. It changed my life.

Don't be afraid to follow your passion. Whatever it is, there's always going to be people saying "Don't do it. There aren't any jobs. It doesn't make money. How are you going to get it?" Forget that. Go for it. I, for example, am currently making the decision of majoring in Theatre in college. I, personally, would rather die before my dream does. I'd rather be practically homeless, yet with some sort of purpose or goal in my life, than make $200,000 a day and hate my life. Follow your passion. It's okay. While all the other people are being driven away from their dream with insecurities and outside opinions, they lean towards the life of not having a passion and living for the benefits, and not for the joy of what they do. They no longer want a job, they just want a paycheck. Those people are the same people who look forward to the weekends when they can get intoxicated and cover their misery with fake happiness. So whatever it is that is your passion, do it with all your heart! As you get older you will realize that most of the adults around you hate their life because they never found their passion and were lied to. They were lied to by being told to work first and play later. By being told that a simple job and money could bring them happiness. The only people who are spiritually fulfilled are the ones who live on their passion. They don't care about housing, money, or materialistic things. They just care about doing what they love to do while everything else takes care of itself. The life they live flies by so quick because of their passion. When I was in Band class, I would sometimes get distracted by my band teacher, Ms. Soebbing, and be mesmerized by the way she conducted. She did it with so much enthusiasm. She was literally lost in the music and looked like she was having the time of her life. She said she'd always liked music and got to the point where she couldn't picture herself doing anything else. So take your Plan B and throw it out the window because you are going to work so hard towards your passion, that you will be unstoppable! Make that decision and follow your heart. If no one has your back, that's okay. It's about you wanting to succeed. Don't be afraid. Love your dream and be yourself. I'd rather die before my dream does. I'd rather live a life with purpose. Prioritize your dreams and your passion, and you'll live a life with something everybody wants: *Meaning*.

Chapter Challenge!

Write down 2 ways you will prioritize your passion for at least 10-15 minutes a day!

If you're a sports person, this could mean practicing every day! If you're artsy, painting or drawing for a while could be the way to go! Want to be a lawyer? Search up a court case! Anything you can do to keep your passion alive. When school is going on, sometimes it can feel like there's no time for anything. But trust me, 10-15 minutes will make a difference!

CHAPTER 3 : SELF LOVE & SELF FORGIVENESS

We live in such an external world. We're always thinking about what other people are thinking. We're concerned about what people say, do, wear, love, hate, and so forth. We're always caught up in things outside our control. For example, in high school I heard a lot of "I'll go if you go!", or "I'll do it if you do it!", and my favorite, "I'll try it if you try it!" We forget to be individuals and live a life that no longer becomes our own. Today's kids love the idea of relationships, but always fail to build a relationship with themselves, which I feel is the most important relationship you could have. I believe that there is a perfect version of you living right inside your heart. A perfect, flawless, beautiful copy of yourself living inside you. Whenever I make decisions I always think about "What would he say?" referring to the David inside of me. I try to bring that perfect David to life everyday by keeping an honest relationship with myself and not letting myself down. I challenge you to do the same thing! There are two great keys to having an amazing relationship with yourself: *Self Love* & *Self Forgiveness.*

Self-Love

Self-love sounds amazing, but how exactly does one do it? The answer is simple, STOP BEING NEGATIVE ABOUT YOURSELF (which is also, way easier said than done). Here's one thing that really frustrates me about today's pop culture: The mockery of misery. Today a kid will see a video of a person falling flat on their face, laugh and say "Same." They'll see a picture of a dead stick figure, laugh and say "Me." As I scrolled through my Facebook feed I would see endless "memes" that made a joke out of depression, suicide, misery, self-doubt, anxiety and failure. I don't find them funny in the slightest bit. Part of that is because I'm a firm believer in the *Law of Attraction*. If all you do is see, hear, and share negativity, you will eventually believe, breathe and *become* negativity. You may have a great life, but if all you're exposed to is humor that shines a light on self-doubt, you will slowly lose confidence in yourself. So if you're a person who makes a joke out of yourself to simply cover up your insecurities, PLEASE STOP. RIGHT NOW. From this point, catch yourself if you have moments of self-doubt, whether it's in a serious or joking manner. Call out your friends if your hear them say things like this, too. There is someone in this world who wishes they could have the life that you have. Don't be whack by dramatizing situations or insecurities when you have all the power to love yourself.

Love every bit of yourself! Own it! Your eye color, skin color, freckles, pimples, hair color, body shape, body weight, personality, everything! Accept yourself for who you are. Loving yourself is not only about accepting, but wanting better for yourself as well. A few months ago I was really chunky. My excuse was that I was method acting to be Shrek in a school play, but really I was just being lazy. But even then, while being a bit bigger than I usually was, I loved myself so much. I made the best out of my chunkiness. After the show ended, I loved myself the way I was and loved myself enough to get back into shape. Not only is this a good mentality for physical weight loss, but for living life in general. You may not be perfect, but love yourself throughout the process of *becoming* perfect. From the beginning all the way to the end, love yourself! Love your past, present and future. There's nothing that scares society more than a confident person. People look at confident people in awe and in jealousy. The jealous people are the type that'll want to bring you down. Stop focusing on external opinions and vibes. Love yourself for who you are and who you'll become. Value your presence and what you stand for. Wake up every morning, look in the mirror and say "I love you!" every day until you believe it, breathe it, and become it! The perfect version inside of you will be very proud!

Self-Forgiveness

If there's anything just as important as self-love, it's self-forgiveness. As I said before, it's okay to be wrong and make mistakes. But we all know it can get tough. There might be moments when we feel like we have no value. We might feel that we'll never be good enough and that we should quit what we're doing right then and there. Whenever you have these moments, you have to tell the perfect version of you living in your heart three words: *I Forgive You*. Always allow yourself a second chance. Remind yourself that it's okay to mess up and that whatever the situation is, it shouldn't prevent you from moving forward. I once had a relationship that didn't end so well. It was the first time I had to do the breaking up. Months later after the relationship ended, the person and I had closure and forgave each other. However, months after our closure I still had this huge chip on my shoulder that kept bothering me and making me feel guilty. It took a long time until I was finally able to forgive myself. Sometimes you'll find yourself in situations where the external problem could already be resolved, but the negative feeling inside you will prevent you from fully moving forward. Self-forgiveness takes time and honesty. I could've dropped out of high school the moment I found out I was failing a class, but I didn't, because I quickly forgave myself and reassured my inner David that I was going to work hard and be okay. Another great way to love and forgive yourself, is by simply being alone.

In order to have a relationship with yourself, you need time with yourself! Take yourself on a date! You don't always have to be around people. If you're with friends 24/7, you eventually lose yourself and also get tired of your friends. It's about finding a balance. I see my group of friends maybe once every two weeks, and every time we hang out, it's pure fun and love. We are so excited to see one another and talk for hours. However, if you hang out with the same person all day, every day, you will reach a certain limit where you'll run out of things to talk about. Start learning how to spend time with yourself. Instead of texting all your friends what they're doing Friday night, have a night to yourself and watch a movie, order a pizza, read a book, do karaoke, something, anything, by yourself. There's a big difference between being lonely and independent. When you're lonely, you really want company (which is a normal thing we all experience, but shouldn't be overdone). If you practice self-love & self-forgiveness you will be independent. You won't mind having a night to yourself because you'll truly enjoy your own company and still have a great time. Isolate yourself a bit and you'll find out who you truly are and find peace within yourself. Isolation can be an hour, or months. It's up to you.

We are all unique in our own way. We belong to so many sub groups like race, age, religion, gender, ect. Even then, everybody is so different and beautiful. Realize that you are one of a kind and that you have tremendous value for the person you are. We live in a time period where social media controls everything and makes a joke out of self-doubt and self-hate. Learn how to love yourself and forgive yourself and you'll see how the world reacts. Some will envy you and some will look up to you. Regardless of what the reaction is, you won't care. You will be too busy trying to please the perfect version inside of you. Don't fall into the traps of negativity. Love yourself, forgive yourself, and you'll see how happy you will become.

Chapter Challenge!

Make a list of 5 things you love about yourself!

These can be physical aspects of you or your personality traits! Things you genuinely love about yourself. Things that make you unique!

Make a list of 2 things you need to apologize to yourself for.

This can be something you might still be holding a grudge about. It can be something you messed up, something you did, said, anything. Something you need to forgive yourself for to get that chip off your shoulder and move forward peacefully.

CHAPTER 4 : GRATITUDE

Being grateful is something we look for in everybody, but rarely do it ourselves. That obviously messes up the balance. For me, *Gratitude* is genuinely appreciating *what* you have, *when* you have it, *where* you have it, whatever the circumstance may be. When being grateful you have to keep three things in mind: *Looking On The Brighter Side*, *Extending Happiness*, and *The Way The Universe Reciprocates*.

Looking On The Brighter Side

At some point, we all come across the "Is the glass half empty or half full?" question. Most of us say the glass is half full and lie to ourselves thinking that we're grateful and optimistic people. The test is just another way to make us feel more positive when we know we're absolutely not. So, here's how being grateful really works. Let's say a person owes you $50, at the moment they can only give you $40. The person is guaranteed to pay you back the full $50, but at this moment they can only give you $40, and the $10 will come later. However, all you can think about and be mad about for the rest of your day is how you're missing $10. You're so caught up in missing those $10 that you forget and are ungrateful for those $40 in front of you. I remember being a kid and having five wrestling toys. My friend who I used to play with only had two. However, he had the two that I didn't have and always wanted. I would spend the night crying thinking about those two wrestlers I didn't have and I would forget about the fact that I simply had more than my friend. As kids we are so accustomed to wanting what we don't have and not acknowledging what we do have. We are accustomed to being ungrateful. This goes to show that the only way to be grateful is to flip a switch and look on the brighter side of the situation.

This chapter is about appreciating the external things in your life with an internal approach. Chapter Three was about you appreciating who are and loving yourself, an internal perspective. This chapter is both internal and external, where I want you to stop focusing on materialistic things you don't have and start paying attention to the essential things you do have and do not give enough credit to. Catch yourself every time you start to complain about something and look on the brighter side. Some complaints might be harder than others. If you catch yourself saying "School is a pain in the butt" think about "At least I'm getting an education." That's pretty broad. If you catch yourself saying "I wanted Lemonade, not water", think about "At least I have something to drink." That's pretty small. No matter how heavy the circumstance is, always look on the brighter side!

Extending Happiness

Being grateful can truly extend your happiness. I'm happy all the time because I truly appreciate the good in all of my surroundings. Part of this is, once again, acknowledging what I do have. That part was easy because of my parents. My parents were born in Mexico in little *Pueblos* where food and clothes were scarce. They had dirt floors and had to go to bathrooms that were a mile away. For them to come to the United States, become citizens and have their own house was considered "making it." Even with their conditions in Mexico, my parents told me that they were always grateful for what they had, even if it was a little. Today I am blessed to be able to have a dream outside of the human essentials. I never had to worry about food or clothes. My parents did, so their dream was to no longer worry about those things. With gratitude and hard work, they made their dream come true, and have given me a life where I can focus on having a dream of my own. This taught me that when we look at things we don't have, we grow sad, angry and envious. But when we look at those who have less than us, we become really grateful of all that we obtain, and perhaps even develop empathy.

When I say be grateful, I'm not saying to be accepting of everything and turn it into a positive. I certainly believe that there is a difference between working hard towards a goal and complaining about stupid things. My parents were grateful for the little they had growing up but also had a goal to create a life that was better for them (Chapter 3). Are you grateful for your old little dying car and are saving up for a new one? That's great! Are you complaining about having to run in gym class? That's really whack. Happiness and gratitude are not the destinations, rather they are the vehicles to accomplishing your dreams. Being grateful can make you so much happier in your day-to-day life. When you look on the bright side and acknowledge what you have that others don't, you'll smile and appreciate more than you've ever done in years.

The Way The Universe Reciprocates

I taught poetry classes to middle school kids since I was a Freshman in high school. I did it for four years and got a great perspective of what teachers have to do in order to make a class function. It was a lot of fun, but it wasn't easy. Those four years taught me that teachers have no idea what children go through, and that kids have no idea what the teachers put up with. Throughout my life I've been very fortunate to have great teachers, many of whom have changed my life in a positive way. My senior year I decided to give back and show some appreciation, since my mom always lectured me about expressing my gratitude. I made a total of 52 little paper quotes that I would give to ten teachers every day. I figured that if teachers are spending their day trying to motivate us, the least I could give back is something small that could motivate them. At the end of the year I even performed a teacher-appreciation poem at one of my high school's faculty meetings. On my last day of school I wrote personal letters thanking ten specific teachers. Some of them expressed how thankful they were for the appreciation and some of them didn't say a word. Regardless of what their reactions were, I was never expecting any. I did everything I did out of *love*. When you do something out of *love*, you don't expect anything in return. When do you something for someone and expect a fair trade, that's called *business*. I wasn't trying to do business with any of my teachers and expecting them to praise me. I was doing the acts of kindness from the bottom of my heart to show appreciation to teachers that helped me out through the years. Your acts of gratitude should always be for the genuine purpose of it, to show appreciation. Your acts and attitudes of gratitude should never come with an expectation of repayment or equal gratitude. That is not the responsibility of the person you are thanking. The universe will take care of that for you.

It was my last week of high school and I had won a raffle. It was a Portillo's gift card that had anywhere between $10-$20 on it. When I got it the first person who came to my mind was a janitor named Pablo Yanez. Earlier in the year, during Speech Season, this janitor would always open a classroom for me to practice in. He would start his shift right after school and always treated me with kindness whenever he saw me. Every Monday during Speech Season he would congratulate me on the tournament that took place over the weekend or asked me how it went. He gave me a special congratulations when I got 3rd Place at the State level. I saw him briefly when I was rehearsing for the Spring Musical and invited him to come see the show. Sure enough, he congratulated me one night after the show. He had gone to see it with his family. So within the last couple days of school I went up to the third floor where he usually worked and thanked him for all his support. I gave him the Portillo's card I had won. The look on his face will be one I will always remember. He was so grateful and told me "I don't care how much is in this card. It's the fact that you thought of me that I am really thankful for. You'll always have a special place in my heart." We embraced one last time and I left with the thought that I was friends with the coolest janitor of my high school.

Right after I gave him the card, I went down to the second floor to see Mr. Malloy, a teacher who I considered as my second father. I loved him to death and would always talk to him after school when I didn't want to go home. I came into his room and he said "I've been waiting for you! I got you something." As a graduation present, he gave me a bible-sized book on the musical *Hamilton* (my favorite play!) that featured the writing process, song lyrics, historical backgrounds, biographies and so much more. The book must've cost a fortune. At that moment, I realized the universe had reciprocated. All I did was give a Janitor a Portillo's card, a sincere "Thank You" speech and hug. In return, I got a huge book that made me fan-girl for five minutes. What you put into the universe, you'll be paid back almost triple. I am a firm believer in karma, both good and bad. If you're always looking for drama, drama will find you three times as much. If you input love and gratitude, the universe will show you love and gratitude three times more. I had a great opportunity of seeing it play out in front of me within five minutes. The universe will reciprocate in minutes, hours, days, weeks, months or years. People will claim they gave up on being nice because they felt they never got anything in return. Well one, they weren't doing it for love, they were doing it for business, and two, the universe takes its time. Patience, faith, love and gratitude have no time limit. They are meant to be practiced endlessly in order to truly enjoy and appreciate the rewards in the end. So start looking on the brighter side to extend your happiness and remember that what goes around, comes around.

Chapter Challenge!

Make a list of 4 people you will give a genuine "Thank You" to in the coming future!

This can be in person, through text, email, phone call or voice mail. My personal favorite is hand-written letters. Those fill a person up with joy. Be grateful and show it!

CHAPTER 5 : ACT & REACT

So far, everything that I've talked about has been internal. Not being whack, being passionate, loving yourself, forgiving yourself, and being grateful. Those are internal things one has to practice. This chapter is focusing on the external and will help you bring those previous chapters to life. Everybody might know about loving yourself and being grateful, but how does one consistently practice it? It's easy! It's all about two things: *Acting & Reacting.*

The Act

1) The Power To Change Your Mood

You are 100% in control of your actions, moods, perceptions and tone of voice. People tend to forget that they have control over these things and let themselves be controlled by an outside force. For example, let's pretend you had an ice cream cone that you waited so long for and was going to guarantee your happiness for the day. Let's also say that the ice cream cone fell onto the floor. Now you're sad. Let's say you had to meet up with your friends five minutes after your ice cream cone fell. Believe it or not, there are some people who will be in the worst mood and take out their frustration and sadness on their friends who had nothing to do with the situation. It's not even a situation in which your friends can help you out with or advise you. It was just a meaningless ice cream cone. People get so caught up over temporary emotions that it effects their long-term mood and disconnects them from society. I can't tell you how many guys have gone quiet and moody when they lost a game in gym class. You have the power to control your own mood. What if after you dropped your ice cream, you remembered that being with your friends made you happy? How about you pretended like it never happened and only focused on having a good time with your friends, instead of being moody all day. I remember going on my overnight Senior Six Flags trip. I got home around 6AM and had to teach a Quinceañera practice at 9AM. With only two hours asleep, I was exhausted. I could've shown up to the practice half dead and said "We'll only practice for half an hour. I'm tired." But I knew that a dance teacher always had to be with high energy and encourage the kids to learn a dance. So I gave it all I had. The practice went on for an hour and a half. The kids had a lot of fun. All I did was take control of my mood and changed it to how I wanted it to be. Even though I was physically dying, I didn't let it stop me from making the best out of my situation. Sometimes you really have to fake it until you make it, which is a form of practice. Changing your mood, voice tone, perceptions and actions can help you change your day, and eventually your life.

2) Respect Is Always A Given

There's this popular thing going around these days about respect "being earned", which I think is the dumbest thing I've ever heard in the history of the world. People say it all the time. "She earned my respect." "He earned my respect." What does that even mean? If you are a decent human being that wants good for the world, you should know that respect is always, automatically, a given. Always. Think about it, if everyone had to earn your respect, that means you'd have to earn everybody's respect, too. Everyone would just be cruel, blank and treating every interaction like an interview. My mother taught me to always give a person respect, especially with strangers because you may not know their story, what they value or what their intentions are. I believe that trust should be earned, not respect. I also believe that respect can only be lost. If you give a person respect to begin with, but then something goes wrong or doesn't click, you can choose not to respect that person. But if the way you start is by having a person earn your respect, it's equivalent to the world turning upside down. I had a friend who I just graduated with that would say "Being nice gets you nowhere." BEING SASSY GETS YOU NOWHERE EITHER. I do agree you have to be ruthless at some point to accomplish your goals, but to not be nice? To not give respect? It's inhumane and immoral. That whole "treat others like you want to be treated", as cheesy as it is, is probably the truest thing you can believe. The universe reciprocates (Chapter 4). If you want to be a person who is admired and praised for being a good person, you need to start by giving people respect. My mom even told me to respect people I didn't like! There's going to be people who you won't want to associate yourself with, but the mature thing to do is to give that person respect, regardless of your feelings towards them. If there's a person you don't like that sits next you in class for a whole year, it's going to be a tough year. But if you treat them with respect and talk to them only when you have to, chances are they'll give you respect back and maybe even want to build a friendship with you. Some of my friends in 8th grade were the biggest trouble-makers in the whole class, but since I treated them with respect, they never picked on me and always defended me. Respect is always a given. It can even be one of the things you start doing to you change your mood!

3) Be The Person You Want To Be

If you're in a party that's really whack and you know you're the outgoing type that wants to get everybody involved, you better put on some music and get jiggy with it! If you see an old lady at Wendy's who is eating by herself and you're the type of person who enjoys a good conversation, get up and go talk to her! Whether she ends up telling you her whole life story or tells you to go away, you acted like the person you wanted to be. I've gone through both scenarios. I've been in restaurants where I talk to the person who is eating along and had them tell me their whole life story, and also been told to go away. Regardless of what the reaction was, I stayed true to the outgoing person that I've always wanted to be. Don't depend on people to give you opportunities to be yourself. Believe, therefore, you are. Some of you might want to be a person that's completely opposite of you. That's okay! Act like the person you want to be and your body and spirit will slowly gravitate to making that possible. Fake it till you make it, in a positive way. Act, be and believe in the person you want to be, and hopefully, all of you want to be good people!

The React

1) Control What Triggers You

You can walk into a place, ready to dance all night and be the life of the party, but let's say that as soon as you walk in someone yells at you and says "Sit your butt down!" Typically, this leads to two things. Either you start throwing punches and get into a fight, or you slowly crawl up in a corner and cry. You can be in a positive mood all the time, but the moment someone triggers you, you might throw that chill vibe out the window and start reacting to the negative trap you just fell into. Being a mascot, I got negative stuff thrown at me all the time. People would tell me to sit down if the team was losing. I ignored them, moved away from them and did my own thing. I controlled the way I reacted by getting away from the negativity and being the person I wanted to be. Reacting doesn't only come with negative things. Sometimes we get too excited and fan-girl over something and do that really high-pitched scream that might not be appropriate depending on where you are. Think about how you react to negative and positive situations. These days people are very sensitive. Anything that is said the wrong way can lead to a mob of people complaining how offended they got. There is certainly a limit where you should step in and defend yourself, but if you're causing a riot because a person called you "weird", they aren't being the whack ones here. Don't get so offended by everything people tell you. Don't be so hyped and happy when people praise you as well. It's a balance of reaction. You have to know your limits for both occasions. My idol in acting and reacting was a Band teacher I had named Mrs. Fitzgerald. She was the type that would be completely calm even if a fire would break out. She'd just laugh and say "Well, time to leave the building." I always admired how calm she would be. There would be moments in class where I would've lost my mind if I was the teacher, but Mrs. Fitzgerald was clearly a master of controlling her reactions, which helped decrease the severity of every situation.

2) Be Appropriate

There will be moments when your trigger limit will be reached and you'll have to react and defend yourself, someone or something. However, always keep in mind that you have to be appropriate. A punch to the face doesn't solve everything. I went to a high school that had a zero tolerance policy. You'd get suspended if you even thought about fighting. Some of our natural and spontaneous reactions end up not being worth it after we see the consequences that come with them. Being appropriate can also be towards the environment that you're in. I believe in being the person you want to be, but if you're always cheery and positive, you might want to tone it down if you're in a funeral home. You might want to whisper in a library and not talk during a movie. This also applies to the shy and timid person who might have to get up if they're at a dance party or at least get on one ride if they're at Six Flags, and we all know that friend who gets yelled at because they can't be serious in an equally serious situation. My mom always told me that there's a time and place for everything. There should always be a balance of being who you are and following the vibe of the environment that you're in, if not, what's the point of being there?

3) Think Before You Speak

Everybody knows this, but nobody does it. When I heard a song by Drake that said "Don't ask for permission, just ask for forgiveness", I thought it was the most irrational thing I had ever heard in my life. Reactions aren't just about physical reactions, but more verbal than anything. People are so quick to talk trash today, you'd think they spend time in the shower practicing negative things to say. In the heat of the moment, we are more likely to say things we don't mean. We can simply avoid those things if we just think before we speak. Half the arguments you have in your lifetime are because of things you didn't say or things you said the wrong way. This also isn't a negative-only thing. When we get so excited we tend to speak really fast, stumble on our words, awkwardly breathe in, and continue talking in a way no one can understand us. Talking and breathing can easily crash against each other. When that happens, remember this cycle: Thought, Inhalation, Speak. First, think of what you're going to say and how you're going to say it. Second, BREATHE IN. Third, breathe out and say what you mean. Simple, right? People are so quick to mess up that cycle and end up being misunderstood, running out of breath or saying something that they didn't mean and getting in trouble. Thinking before you speak can save you a million *I'm Sorry*'s and *I didn't mean that, can you forgive me?*'s. Thinking before you speak can help you explain something or even give a presentation in class. When I was in Speech Team, my coach Ms. Prochaska taught me the art of breathing. When you have control of your breath, you control your heart beat. It makes it easier for your mind to process what you want to say and how you want to say it. Just try it! It won't hurt!

You have the power to change your mood. Start giving respect to everybody and being the person you want to be. Be careful about what triggers you, what's appropriate, and always think before you speak! By paying attention to how you act and react, you will be 10x more successful in not being whack, being passionate, loving and forgiving yourself and being grateful!

Chapter Challenge!

Write down 3 personality traits that you wish to obtain!

I wasn't always outgoing or cheery. It definitely took some practice. Write down some traits you would like to have. They don't always have to be extroverted traits. It can be being more nonchalant, serious, wise, clean, or confident. Outgoing and cheery are my personal favorites.

Write down 3 things that trigger you and how you will work on reacting to them!

Ever since I've tried this, it's really hard for me to fall into a negative trap. I took what used to make me feel offended and practiced reacting to it in positive and appropriate ways. Write down what triggers you and a way to decrease your immediate reaction. It could be as simple as breathing, having an appropriate response ready, a joke, or simply ignoring it.

CHAPTER 6 : FINDING YOUR ESCAPE

I believe in taking breaks. Breaks are meant for one to heal and recover, but never meant for one to stop. Within these little breaks you have though, it's always a great time to go to your escape. Finding your escape is having something to go to when you're stressed out, getting away from a problem, or simply taking a break from so much that has been going on. Your escape serves two purposes: *Staying At Peace With Yourself* and *Self Dependency*.

Staying At Peace With Yourself

Taking a break doesn't always have to be from something negative. It isn't always to avoid stress or drama. Sometimes you can just be really tired from a tight schedule and want a break. The escape itself can be just about anything. It can be watching a movie, a TV series, playing with a Rubix Cube, playing with a slinky, doing math problems, drawing a picture, writing poetry, anything. Your escape doesn't have to be your passion. If it is, that just makes life a bit easier. But for example, I once had a doctor who told me her escape was photography. She said she loved her job but would need a break when the stress would build up. After taking some great pictures and sharing them with friends or social media, she would feel relieved and get back to the job she loved. Your escape should be about feeling peaceful. That's what photography did to my doctor. It brought her back to level one. Your escape should feel like a big deep breath of relief. Your whole body should be taking a breath and grounding itself. If your escape is bringing you more stress or making you think too much, it's probably not for you. For starters, I always recommend music. It's the easiest way to go. People say music can change your mood, but I disagree. I think music only enhances your mood. If you're feeling great, you're going to play some Earth, Wind & Fire. If you're feeling sad, The Fray might be on your playlist. If you reverse those two moods with those two bands, you'll be asking to turn it off. However, only in the case of needing a break or feeling the need to be relaxed, listen to some mellow and soothing music. I'm sure it'll work. Just feel your body take one big breath and you'll feel recovered and healed. Sometimes a really good nap comes right after too.

Self-Dependency

Regardless of what your escape is, it should always be a thing you do alone. Here's something I learned a while ago: *A good friend will be there for you, a great friend will teach you how to be there for yourself.* There are some great friends out there who will be there for you at the sound of a call or text, which is great. Even then, you still have to practice the ability to be there for yourself. There are many times when my breaks include hanging out with my friends and having a good time. A majority of my breaks, however, are me going to my escape. If your only escape is your friends, what will you do when they're not available? This is why one needs to practice *Self Dependency*. Finding your escape makes it 10x more easier. Back in 8th grade, I felt like I didn't have anyone to talk to. I had friends here and there, sat at the big lunch table, but still felt empty within the conversations that I was having with them. Since I didn't have anybody to go to, I took a big interest in poetry. I started writing every day and became really decent at it. I felt at peace with myself and no longer needed attention from other people. I would spend my weekends writing. As I got older and started seeing people posting paragraphs on Facebook looking for fake sympathy, I was happy that I was able to find my escape of poetry. Poetry allowed me to express myself openly. Instead of getting fake sympathetic comments or friends just comparing my story to theirs, I was received with applause everywhere I performed and even received comments like "You said everything I've ever wanted to say", all because I was self-dependent.

Be there for yourself more than anybody else. Poetry and music saved my life. Don't depend on other people to be there for you all the time because there will be a moment where they won't, or they simple won't understand your situation. Start accepting the concept of being independent. This chapter is for that 10% of your life when you'll be taking a break. Breaks come at different intervals. I'm the type that'll go all out for three months and take a break for one week. Some of you might go for two weeks and take a break for one day. Find your escape and be self-dependent. Recovering and healing will progress 10x faster and smoother. Take a deep breath, find your escape, recover, and go!

Chapter Challenge!

Write down 2 things you go to, or will go to, when you take a break!

Remember! This shouldn't include any friends or being on your phone! Find a hobby, read a book, anything that'll make your body take a big deep breath and be ready to go live life again.

CHAPTER 7 : UNDERSTANDING

We live in an era where everybody wants to be right and prove the other person wrong. We choose not to listen anymore and just want everything to be our way. We can see that within today's political and diversity issues. People just want to debate and win instead of understand and compromise. However, being able to understanding isn't that easy either. When you practice the art of understanding, you have to keep in mind three things: *Keeping Yourself Concrete & Your Mind Fluid, Knowing Before Judging*, and *Practicing Empathy.*

Keeping Yourself Concrete & Your Mind Fluid

I identify myself as a young, straight Mexican-American male. How is it possible that I can be friends with a 30-year-old African-American woman who's gay? On paper, one might ask "That's a friendship?" Perhaps the lady and I like the same band, or the same book, or just have awesome conversations about the weather. Even though our labels are completely different, we can still communicate, be friends and understand each other. I have co-workers at my job who are way older than me but yet we still get along because of common interests. Sounds like common sense right? Well believe it or not, there's a lot of people who don't know how, or simply don't want to do that. There are many people who restrict themselves from social interactions and only talk to people that are just like them. I know Mexican-American kids my age who talk to their parents in English when their parents only speak Spanish. I know kids my age who cannot talk to adults because they don't know how or they simply don't want to. If all you know is who you are, you are limiting and preventing yourself from getting to know a bigger world around you. That's why it's important to keep yourself concrete, but keep your mind fluid. Keeping yourself concrete means knowing who you are. What are your labels? What are your values? What do you say no and yes to? That's being concrete, nothing changing who you are. Keeping your mind fluid is being able to understand other things or people that are different from who you are. There are a lot of people who are so concrete that think everything they believe in is correct, therefore, everything they don't believe in, they reject. There are also people who are so fluid that they basically don't have a personality of their own and live the life of a follower. They like and dislike what everybody else does but never form a firm individual opinion. There always has to be a balance.

For example, a couple weeks ago I went to the Pride Parade where they celebrate the LGTBQ community. It was filled with bright colors, people dancing, smiling and just wanting to have a good time. It was incredible. Now, do I belong to that community? I don't. However, I *understand* the movement and their intentions. From what I saw at Pride, I understand that the community simply wanted to be happy with who they were and be accepted. At the end of the day, most of the people in the world, regardless of their sexual orientation or preference, just want to be happy with who they are be accepted too. Even though I am not a part of their community, I was able to keep my mind fluid and become a strong advocate for them because I agreed with their intentions. Understanding can help strengthen, weaken and change perceptions. Keep yourself concrete and know who you are, but keep your mind fluid and be willing to learn and understand why people are the way they are.

Knowing Before Judging

How exactly does one keep their mind fluid? How does one make their way into learning about different kinds of people? We hear that cheesy saying "Don't judge a book by its cover" all the time. But to be honest, that is something we will never get rid of. It is the most natural thing to do when you meet someone for the first time. It's what leads to a first impression. Everyone is always going to judge someone by their cover, and it's okay. But here's where you can apply a change. As soon as you have your first impression about a person, you need to flip a switch inside your head and remind yourself that you don't know their *story*, their *values* and their *intentions*.

Back in Freshman year of high school, I remember the Travon Martin case being a huge deal. I didn't know much about it and thought it was just another negative thing on the news. I didn't care so much. A year later I was at a Poetry camp at UIC and was in a group discussion with 50 other kids who were primarily African American. As we were going around the circle they were sharing personal stories about being victims of Chicago violence and police discrimination. Some stories were broader than others. Tears ran down the faces of many. I couldn't believe my eyes and ears. These weren't stories that made it to the news, these were just stories from the everyday life for some of those kids. From that moment on I understood why police brutality was a serious issue. I understood why mothers gave their child a blessing every time before they went out. I understood how discrimination can affect someone's perceptions and actions. I understood why "Black Lives Matter." I *understood*. When we see something on the news we are so quick to judge and not go further into learning about the situation. I was there listening to personal stories that helped me understand what people valued, what they feared and what they would stand up for. People today are so ignorant and refuse to understand why something is the way it is. Not many people know why black and brown people live in parts of the city that they do. People think that it's their choice. Not many people know the history of discrimination and oppression that forced black and brown people to live in isolated communities with few resources and poor infrastructure. Kids today are born into a lifestyle and think "This is who I am, therefore, all I will ever be" and grow up not being taught about diversity or about the different types of people around them.

People ask questions but never do research to find out the answer. Why would a person want to change their gender? Why would a person change their skin color? Why would a person commit suicide? Why would a person want to leave home? Why would a person want to write a book? Why is that person happy all the time? All of these questions have specific answers but nobody is willing to figure them out. Everybody just judges within their first impression and let it be. Understanding isn't just about accepting. Understanding is learning the why and how and then forming your opinion based on your research. There are plenty of cruel things in the world that you might learn about and understand and still have the same opinion you started with. That's okay. Just because you understand it, doesn't mean it's okay and acceptable. That's more for bigger issues that would be immoral to defend.

Understanding is also just about keeping peace. You don't have to agree with the idea being presented, but at least respect it. My key factor is this: *If it doesn't affect you or anybody else, who cares?* I, for example, am not a fan of tattoos. I would never get one. But do I have hard feelings for those that do? Of course not! It's their body and it doesn't affect me at all! If a friend asks me to go out for Chinese food, knowing I don't like Chinese food, I might say something since their decision is affecting me directly. Simple examples, but the concept can also apply to bigger things.

Nowadays no one wants to be labeled, which I agree with. But I do think that you should pick your own labels. If you don't belong to anything, then who are you? People try to be slick and say they don't see or believe in race, religion or sexuality. But if they have to acknowledge those labels, doesn't that mean they exist? Labels are something we will never demolish. Trying to pretend they're not there isn't going to solve anything. I used big labels in this chapter because they're regularly brought up in today's pop culture world where everybody is either trying to take pride in who they are, or trying to run away from labels all together. Meeting people will not always come down to these labels. It could be as minor as understanding why someone likes a genre of music, a style of poetry or a sport. I used big labels because we all belong to something and at the same time are unique in our own way. It's being able to acknowledge and accept each other's differences and forming a bond and friendship based off of the simple concept of understanding. The best form of understanding leads to another thing: *Empathy*.

Developing Empathy

The world needs empathy more than ever before. Sympathy is feeling bad for something or someone, which is still needed very much. However, empathy is the simple ability to understand something's or someone's feelings and emotions. I practiced that all the time in Theatre. Our responsibility when we got the role of a character was to understand the character's feelings and to figure out how to interpret those emotions through dialogue, movement or song. Practicing empathy starts all the way from the beginning. You keep yourself concrete, keep your mind fluid, learning before judging, and within that process of learning and understanding, you will develop empathy.

I remember walking home one day from work next to an old African-American man. All I did was ask him "What music did you listen to while growing up?" For the next 30 minutes he sang me a song, told me his whole life story, told me his concerns, prides, fears and triumphs. By the time we got to his bus stop I had developed simple empathy. I understood what he felt and why he felt that way. Developing empathy can be done in a simple conversation, watching a play, or watching a documentary. When you develop enough empathy, it gets harder to get mad. When I see a child being a brat I don't think that they're a bad kid. The first thing I think about is that there's probably some parenting issues at home. I understand why the kid is behaving that way. It gets harder to get mad when you start realizing everything has a reason. Understanding can decrease anger, judging, and ultimately, discrimination.

What I recommend to do to start practicing understanding is to build personal connections with people who are different from you. I have friends that you wouldn't possibly think we'd have anything in common. It can start out by having a common interest in a book or a movie. Start expanding your social interactions with people who are not exactly like you. Not every single YouTube video will help you understand other people. Watching the news is a terrible idea and don't even get me started on those "BuzzFeed" or "NowThis" videos on Facebook. Don't listen or watch sources that are completely bias to one perspective. The best perspectives are always the personal ones. So go out there and make friendships with people and learn their story. Some of them will be eager to tell you everything, some of them will tell you to leave them alone. Regardless of what it is, you'll know that you're putting in an effort to make a world a better place by being willing to learn about and understand people instead of judging or stereotyping them. At the end of the day, everybody just wants to be happy with who they are, be accepted, be loved and understood.

Chapter Challenge!

Write down the labels you identify yourself with!

This can be as broad as race, age group, sexual orientation, ect., and it can be as small as Bookworm, Hip Hop Head, Theatre Kid, Batman Fan, any and all labels broad and small!

Write down some labels you wish you learn more about!

Think about labels that you would want to do research on or make a friend with those labels. It can be broad like learning about a different culture, or small like a different genre of music. Think of any labels, big or small, that you know will help you understand something new at the end of the day.

CHAPTER 8 : DO IT YOURSELF

I've said it once and I'll say it a thousand more times: *We live in an external world.* We wait for things to happen to us, we react the way we're expected to and go on with the flow. It gets harder and harder to make conscious individual decisions. I can't tell you how many situations I've been in where something easy could've gotten done if someone just stood up and did it, but never did because everybody just looked around to see who was going to do it. Psychology even calls this the *Bystander Effect.* In life, you have to remember that you always have to do it yourself, regardless of what the situation might be. In school, there would be countless people complaining about waking up early in the morning to take the school bus. I would always think about my friend Prince Washington, who would have to take two CTA buses in order to get to school and back home every day. He told me he loved our school so much that he was willing to travel for two hours to make it on time, while other people complained about having to wake up 30 minutes before school. My friend Prince knew that in order to succeed and make the best of what he had, he had to "Do It Himself."

There are a lot of creative little projects you can find to do online called DIY Projects (Do It Yourself Projects). Those Projects consist of you gathering everyday materials and building a product on your own. Take that same concept and apply it to your life. When you "Do

It Yourself", you have to keep in mind two things: *Doing It Every Day* and *Doing It For Your Dreams*.

Doing It Every Day

The other day I was with my friend playing basketball at the park. I couldn't help but notice maybe 15 empty water bottles around the grass near the basketball court. I could've left the bottles there and ignored the problem. I could've gone to the office building and told them that there was trash and that somebody should pick it up. I could've put the mess on my Snapchat and said "What a messy park." I could've done so many things except directly contribute to the problem. Instead, I picked up all 15 bottles and threw them away. I acknowledged the problem, expected no one to help me, and did it myself. It's little things like that that you have to keep in mind when "Doing It Yourself" every single day. I always found it funny when my mom would call me on her phone to come upstairs and give her the TV control when it was only two feet away from her. It's the little things we fail to practice every day that eventually makes us lazy and dependent. We fail to practice small things like throwing our own trash away, cleaning our room, washing our clothes, getting up and getting our own drink, asking our own questions and making our own choices.

Doing it for yourself is not only *for* yourself. Sometimes it can come with responsibility. If you see an old lady pass out at the train station in front of a lot of people, don't wait for someone to come help her just because there's a lot of people around, go help her yourself! If you have the capability to help out during an emergency, go ahead and do it! Many crimes and injuries have occurred because of the bystander effect. Everybody sees what's going on, but no one does anything about it. The bystander effect isn't only in emergencies either. I can't tell you how many parties I've been to where I opened up the dance floor because everybody was looking around waiting to see who'd get up first. If you know you're the outgoing type, go ahead and start the dance. Do it yourself! No one is going to do your homework for you. Do it yourself! At some point no one is going to cook for you. Do it yourself! No one is going to make you lose weight. Do it yourself! Take ownership of your actions and aspirations in your everyday life and practice it. People complain until someone does it for them, don't do it at all, or do it with agonizing pain of laziness. Don't be like those people! If you practice doing little things by yourself, you'll be able to practice it at a higher level, like defending someone in the need of help, advocating for someone who doesn't have a voice, standing up for what you believe in, asking questions or being able to help out during an emergency. When you practice doing it yourself, your confidence only gets bigger and bigger along with the willingness to take on responsibility. Nowadays people treat responsibility like cooties, so you'll be ahead of the game by a thousand!

Doing It For Your Dreams

Once you practice doing it yourself every day, you can start applying it to your goals and dreams. This so crucial because not many people are going to help in making your dreams come true, either because they're working on their own dream, don't care about yours, or don't think yours is possible. In fact, there was one brutal thing that I learned this year: *No one cares about your ideas.*

During my Sophomore year in high school I had a great idea to produce original songs that would feature students from the choir, orchestra, band and art departments. I went to my school's Activities Director to tell him about the idea. He loved it, but that's it, he just loved it. He would tell me "Yeah, let's talk about it later!" I would go into his office almost every day just to hear "I love it. Talk to the teachers about it!" As much as he liked my idea, deep down inside, he didn't care about it, but not because he didn't like me or didn't like what I wanted to do, but he simply had much bigger things to worry about than a Sophomore with an idea. After I got the hint, I decided to do it myself. I wrote and produced a song, talked and teamed up with individual musicians, singers and artists and completed a song within four weeks that featured 20 students. I also teamed up with the school's amazing Social Media Director, Mr. Feltman, and had him make a school "Soundcloud" account and have the song posted right on the front page of the school website. That same day I went to the Activities Director and heard the same "I love the idea! Go talk to..." and before he could finish I said "Well, check the homepage. It's up and running." He looked at me with a shocked face. From that day forward he took all my ideas very seriously and even invited me to plan out and host events. He didn't care about my idea, but once I showed him the product and the blueprint of how I did it, he gave me his full attention. No one will ever care about your ideas. Do it yourself and present the product or blueprint of your idea, which is the only way people will take you seriously. Once I started producing songs for my school I had many students tell me they could rap or sing or had an idea for this and that. I would nod and ask them to show me but they could never actually do it. They just had ideas, no blueprints or products, just ideas.

You don't have to tell your dreams and aspirations to everyone. Lin Manuel Miranda, the composer of the hit musical *Hamilton*, told his idea for the musical to his personal friends who all laughed at him. After that, he isolated himself and even skipped out on friend's birthday parties to work on his musical. When he showed those same friends demos of the first couple songs, they looked at him and knew he had something special. Products and blueprints are taken seriously. Ideas are often laughed at. Almost every single invention in history had someone who didn't think it was possible. One of my favorite rappers, J. Cole, said it in one of his songs, "If they don't know your dreams, then they can't shoot them down." Artists work on albums years before they even release the first single. No one knows that I'm writing this book that you're reading right now. If I told them my idea people might say "What do you know about writing a book? Or about life?" But if I were to show them an 100-page book, they'd look at me with wide eyes.

We were all babies at one point that wanted to walk without the help of anyone. We'd roll over, get up, and start running until we fell or had our parents and siblings chasing after us hoping we wouldn't get hurt. We'd do it all ourselves. It should be any different when we get older. We should always have dedication and grit to bring our dreams to a reality. It starts off by practicing little things in our everyday life and things we would normally complain about or wait for someone else to do. By practicing the small stuff, we can then apply them to bigger actions and be ready to take on the beast of responsibility. You do it yourself and for your dreams, which nobody has to know about until you have the product or blueprint. Whether you're finding your escape or doing it yourself, it's all about self-dependency. Stop waiting for permission or for someone to give you attention for picking up an empty water bottle or speaking up for yourself. You don't need permission to be a good human being, to be grateful, helpful, or to follow your dreams. Just do it yourself, and you'll see the difference.

Chapter Challenge!

Make a list of 3 things you will start doing yourself!

1) Something you can easily do for yourself every day
Ex. Washing your own dish, cleaning your room, working out, ect.

2) Something you can do around you (At home or in your community)
Ex. Picking up trash, organizing clothes, watering plants, ect.

3) Something bigger you want to accomplish
Ex. Speaking up for yourself, finding a job, mastering a skill, ect.

CHAPTER 9 : PROCRASTINATION

We've all experienced that deep sigh after nothing gets done. We all know how crazy it can get when we're rushing to do something in the last minute (aka my entire high school career). We all procrastinate. It's perfectly normal. When we think of procrastination, we simply think of putting something off to the side, wasting our time, and then rushing to complete the task. Although that is a form of it, there's another one that many people don't notice. It's called *priority procrastination.*

Sometimes you don't get things done because they're simply not important to you or you have other priorities. When I had Theatre and school going on at the same time, I didn't do my homework because I was lazy, but I just didn't care about it enough compared to Theatre. Procrastination is not based on the waste of time, but simply the use of time. When thinking about procrastination, keep in mind two things: *Procrastination In Your Daily Life* and *Procrastination Towards Your Dreams.*

Procrastination In Your Daily Life

My favorite antonym for the word "procrastination" would be the word "now." The opposite of procrastination is getting stuff done in the moment in front of you. This is easier said than done because of another word: *Laziness*. Our bodies are designed to reject any kind of discomfort. This can include running a mile, getting up after sitting too long, or the worst one, getting out of bed in the morning. We don't want to do any of those things and we sometimes procrastinate for hours until we actually do some of these actions. Even when we actually do them, we make sure we complain the whole way through. The only way to truly be successful and be productive every day is to get up and do what you have to do. It starts with the little things in your everyday life. This chapter goes hand in hand with Chapter 8, Doing It Yourself. Throw the garbage away, RIGHT NOW. Take a shower, RIGHT NOW. Clean your room, RIGHT NOW. Do your homework, RIGHT NOW. Play a board game, RIGHT NOW. There's so many things you can do in one day, even in one hour. We make the mistake of stalling for so long and wasting time. There's been so many times where my mom tells me to do a chore and I'll respond with "I'll do it right now" and end up forgetting about it, followed by getting yelled at two hours later. We say "I'll do it later" to homework, cleaning our room, calling our friends, making appointments, even to filling out college or job applications. We waste so much time doing senseless things like binge watching 15 episodes of Netflix, taking 6-hour naps, or scrolling through our social media for three hours. What one needs to practice is the art of *now*.

Whatever task you have to do, try to attack it and fully focus on it at the moment you receive it. It doesn't always have to be with chores and responsibilities. It can be deciding where you want to go with your friends, working out in the morning, satisfying your craving of a burger, dancing at a party, ect. Sometimes we spend so much time thinking that it prevents us from *doing*. Other times we get too confident. I would make To-Do lists and would have half of it done by noon. I would say to myself "I'm doing great. I'm going to take a nap." It would be dark when I woke up and suddenly I was extremely behind on my list. We make the terrible mistake of rushing at night, sleeping late, waking up late, feeling tired all day, and rushing at night again, creating an unhealthy cycle. Here is the perfect way to practice defeating procrastination: *The 5-Second Rule*. Author Mel Robbins said that you have a 5-Second window from thought to action. If you have an idea or intention, you have five seconds before you actually do it, or don't do it at all. Use it for everything! Don't want to get up in the morning? Count down from five and get up. Don't want to start washing the dishes? Count down from five. Want to talk to your intimidating teacher? Five Seconds! By adding pressure to yourself, it'll create a self-discipline in you that'll defeat any type of procrastination you encounter in your day-to-day life. Pay attention to the little things you put aside every day for "later" and do them at that moment. The rich man and the poor man both have 24 hours in a day, but depending on how they use their time, both of their lives can change for the better, or for the worse.

Procrastination Towards Your Dreams

When I was a little munchkin I always hated the question "What do you want to do when you grow up?" When I was in 5th grade, I started asking myself "What can I do right now?" Our whole lives we make the mistake of wanting to master something before we can show it off. I know kids who won't play pick-up basketball games because they think they're not "good enough." Other people who won't try to speak the new language they're learning because they're "still getting used to it." You don't have to be an expert to express yourself. The only way to become an expert is to learn. When I asked myself in 5th grade what I could do, I went to my passion, music. Within a year I was fortunate enough to have a laptop, a microphone and some producing and recording software. I would produce and compose song after song thinking they were amazing because they came straight from my heart. Years later when I listen to those songs now, I think that they're horrible. However, when I was younger I thought they were amazing and shared them with my friends and social media. I didn't master the art of music production and recording in order to put out songs. I just did it. By making mistakes I was able to learn and adjust. Now, I love the music I compose because I've learned so much. If I didn't release those terrible songs, I wouldn't have learned what to do and what not to do.

When you start prioritizing your passion, *Priority Procrastination* can come into play. You don't have to graduate college in order to start your dream career. You can start making your dreams come true by using the time you have in front of you. If you want to be a doctor, volunteer or apply for an internship at a hospital. Want to be a lawyer? Ask if you can see a case at the courthouse. Want to be a dance teacher? Host dance classes and invite your friends and family. A lot of people make the mistake of choosing a career that they find interesting but have no idea how it works because they've never been exposed to it. Finding and creating opportunities are the difference makers when making your dreams come true. Learning as you go is just as important. I don't know anything about writing books, however, I'm learning about it as I write these chapters. Don't worry about mastering something. That takes years. Don't procrastinate when trying to do something that you love. Prioritize your self-expression. From chapters before, you know that you have to love yourself and do everything yourself. We as humans are tormented with the thought of "not being good enough." That mentality will get you absolutely nowhere. Curiosity, willingness and determination will open your eyes and perception to what's possible. Will you skip homework assignments like me? I hope not. But prioritizing your passion and actually doing it will put you ahead of everybody.

Your dreams can turn into a reality faster than you can imagine. It's all about using your time. Practice the 5-Second rule and turn those thoughts and intentions into action. When you have enough self-discipline, apply your mentality to bigger goals. You don't have to be an expert to express yourself in any field. You have to start somewhere, and most importantly, you have to start NOW.

Chapter Challenge!

List 3 things you will no longer procrastinate in!

These should be 3 things you do in your day -to-day life! It can be based on responsibility and chores, or based on self-care and fun!

List 3 ways you can live your dream today!

What are 3 ways in which you can get closer to your dream? What opportunities can you take advantage of today?

CHAPTER 10 : FIND YOUR MENTOR

As I've stated before, self-dependency is very important. That's what chapters 6 & 8 really focus on. But of course, there are going to be moments when you're going to need some help. Who and where you get that help from is extremely important! This is when you have to find a *Mentor*. A teacher is someone who guides you step by step how to accomplish a certain task or skill or to think a certain way. A mentor is more of an "advice" person. However, the advice they give could be the most valuable thing that can influence your life. That's why it's important finding the right one. I've been very lucky to have amazing people in my life who have shared their wisdom and have guided me into becoming the person I am today. They all have two things in common: They want what is best for me and support me in my dreams and aspirations. The best way to find and adopt mentors is to do three things: *Don't Go To Your Friends*, *Find Someone Old And Wise*, and *Give Back.*

Don't Go To Your Friends

A common mistake that the youth makes today is going to their friends when they need some advice or help. Don't get me wrong, I've have many great friends who always have the right thing to say and the right way to say it. You might have some friends who are always there for you if you need something. However, sometimes making a decision is harder than just getting the opinion of your friends. The typical thing that happens is that they interrupt you and start talking about their situation that was similar to yours, or the advice they give you is biased to what they've experienced at the moment. For example, If someone needs advice on whether they should stay in a relationship they're in and go to their friend who just got cheated on, chances are their friend will tell them that relationships are a complete waste of time. If you ask your friend for financial advice, the one who is working, making good money and didn't go to college, they might tell you to quit school and get right to work. When you go for advice to people your age, they'll just reiterate the decisions they made in a situation like yours. The problem with that is that there's no room to see long-term effects like satisfaction or regret. I go to my friends when I'm looking for a distraction. If I'm feeling stressed, I go to my friends and forget about it for a while. If I'm feeling down, I go to my friends for comfort. But when it comes down to pondering a big decision or analyzing a situation, your friends might not be the people to go to. You and your friends are basically figuring out life at the same time. They don't know any more than you do. So the next time you have a situation and want to forget about it, find your escape or go out with your friends. But if you're really looking for some advice, go to your mentor.

Find Someone Old And Wise

When you think of mentor, you might be thinking of Mr. Feeny from the TV show "Boy Meets World", or Master Shifu from the movie "Kung Fu Panda." That's exactly what a mentor should be. They don't have to be that old, but definitely older than you. You can decide the age gap you want. I'm an 18-year-old that's mentoring 16-year-olds. You get the point. Back when I was in 7th grade I didn't eat in the lunchroom because I didn't know where I fit in. I wasn't as social as I am today. I had friends, but not the "let's talk and hang out every day" type of friends. I went to my Art teacher, Ms. Custodio, and asked her if I could do some work for her during lunch. She kindly said yes. We'd talk here and there and shared a passion for music. Every Friday she'd give me a CD containing an old album. They'd range from Rock to Hip Hop music. Within the music she gave me I started developing confidence and self-dependency. I no longer felt the need to fit in. Music was all I needed. My art teacher mentored me with few words, but with a lot of sounds. On the last day of school, she gave me about 15 CD's. She was the first teacher that I felt actually cared about me.

When I was in 8th grade, things had changed a bit. With the confidence I developed and with the process of following my passion, I joined the basketball team and started sharing my music. My friends became the trouble makers who played basketball and liked Rap music. I respected them and they respected me (Chapter 5). But one day during Parent-Teacher Conferences, my homeroom teacher, Mr. Kelly, sat me down and told me a story of him having a friend who was nothing like him. His friend was a trouble maker who didn't end up going the right route. He told me that the night his friend made a big mistake was the same night my teacher rejected the offer of going to a party. He told me that I had a lot of potential and to be careful of who I associated myself with. He warned me of the habits that could be picked up. The look in his eyes showed nothing but care. He truly believed in me and took the time to have a one-on-one conversation with me that changed my life.

In my Junior year of High School I was pondering on ending a year-long relationship with my at-the-time girlfriend. Things weren't going so well and I needed some advice. I went to my favorite literature teacher, Mr. Malloy, the same teacher who gave me the *Hamilton* book (Chapter 4). What I loved most about his way of giving advice was the possible scenarios he would play out for me. He would give me a huge list of pros and cons. He would tell me what to be careful about and what to consider. At the end he would always reminded me that he would support me. With his help, I was able to leave the relationship I was in and find my happiness again.

A great mentor can provide you things that these three different teachers did for me. They can help you escape, they can tell you what not to do, they can give you the pros and cons, and ultimately, just support you. When you go to someone older, you can practically hear the long term effects that they've experienced with the type of situation that you had. My art teacher listened to music like she depended on it. My 8th grade teacher really missed his friend. My Literature teacher probably had to break up with a girlfriend once too. A great mentor can share with you advice that can possibly prevent or duplicate an experience. Finding an older and inspiring mentor can change your life with all the wisdom you can receive from them. Not everybody that's older than you can be a mentor. It takes them wanting the best for you and truly supporting you that'll make it obvious.

How do you find a mentor? What should you look for in them? Finding a mentor is almost like buying a car or a house. You have to look for specific traits. Your mentor does not have to be perfect, for they are just another human being after all. Your mentor has to have a mentality or traits that you admire. I typically have two questions to evaluate a potential mentor. The first one I ask is "What are your three keys to success?" Their three keys can show you what type of person they are and their work ethic. The second one is "If you could have dinner with five people, dead or alive, who would they be?" With that question, you can see who and what they admire, and maybe what they even value. I remember asking these two questions to the new Superintendent that my high school hired, Dr. Kingsfield. Her answers were so inspiring that I knew they had hired the right person. So go out there and find your mentor! Consider yourself a "Cory Mathews" or a "Po." If you can't find one, just read this book again!

Giving Back

Mentoring is not just a one-way road. Why do you think I'm writing this book? I've had many mentors in my life inspire me and fill me with knowledge and wisdom, and along with that came the desire to give back. Since I started high school I was teaching the fundamentals of Slam Poetry to 6th, 7th & 8th Graders. Some kids were only a year younger than me, but always listened with open ears. I taught poetry for four years and even took some students to compete in poetry competitions. In high school I had a group of students who I would mentor and give advice to here and there. For a while I had a Facebook group of about 30 kids who I would lecture and mentor because I genuinely believed in all of them. I was the kid that my teachers saw potential in. I was the "light in the classroom" that was acknowledged. I try acknowledge that lit within someone else every day. I can always tell if there's a spark within a kid that has to be ignited. I tell them they have potential and take them under my wing. If you know a little boy or girl who has this spark, offer them your help or give them some advice. There are many people who care about you, and there's nothing more positive than giving some of that care back to someone younger, who could eventually want to be just like you.

There's nothing better than having someone who always has your back. That person doesn't, and really shouldn't always be a friend, but rather someone a bit older who has lived long enough to tell you the good and bad. My life has changed by listening to mentors tell me stories of their lives. Find someone who wants the best for you and genuinely supports you. Sometimes those people are the ones who give us advice once a year, give us that care that no one else does, or pushes us harder than anybody else. The same help they give you should be equally given out to someone younger than you. The world is a chain of passing down wisdom and knowledge. Make sure you're getting it from the right person, and given it back to the right person too.

Chapter Challenge!

Make a list of 3 people you have, or plan to adopt, as mentors!

Try to make sure these are people who you can talk to face-to-face in some way. Admiring a celebrity is nice, but you can't go to them when you want some help. These people can be family members, local business owners, part of your school staff, or people you find in the phone book who sound pretty successful. Go find a mentor!

CHAPTER 11 : RELATIONSHIPS

Early on in this book I talk about building a relationship with yourself. I talk a lot about internal concepts like self-love, self-forgiveness and self-dependency. In this chapter we will be addressing the relationships that we have in the external world. Who and how we associate with is just as important as our internal concepts. This chapter will give you an insight on what to look out for and how to react. As humans we have a natural inclination to socialize, regardless of how introverted we are. The relationships you build with people can influence your everyday actions and mentality. Here are the relationships you have to analyze: *Friendships (Toxic vs. Helpful), Family (Degrading vs. Supporting)* and *Romantic Relationships (Possessive vs. Comfort)*.

Friendships (Toxic vs. Helpful)

What makes a person a potential "friend" is the minimal standard of respecting and liking each other. There are many levels in the world of friendships. There's the friend that you only see in the hallways for about two minutes, and there's the friend who is practically your brother or sister. Regardless of what level of friendship you have with the person, the minimal standard is always there. But here's when things can get tricky. People do not realize how a simple friendship can influence your life. You can ignore or block out any stranger, but when you adopt someone as a friend, you're more open to be influenced by them. Sometimes, those influences can be really toxic, or really helpful.

I remember having a friend in high school who was so sweet and kind. She was the nicest person you could ever meet and was always up for anything. This, however, was only when one was alone with her. As kind as she was, she had terrible friends. Her friends were two girls who had bad attitudes and thought everything was whack or too cheesy. They could suck the life out of you with one complaint. I started noticing that whenever I was alone with my friend, she was such a cool person. But when we were in public and around her friends, she would want to isolate herself or not want to participate in what the group was doing. She would have a snarky attitude and negative vibe. Year after year, it only got worse. This only shows how a friendship you have could be toxic and influence you without even noticing. It made my friend go from being a super nice person to a super negative-nelly.

People also make the mistake of blaming time for keeping an unhealthy friendship. I once addressed the same friend and asked her about why she hung out with such negative people. Her response was that they were the first people she made friends with in high school, therefore, would feel bad if she just left them. Time has absolutely no factor in a good friendship. People think it does, but it really doesn't. I knew another friend who had a "best friend," but they had such an average friendship. They called each other best friends because they knew each other since 4th grade. During our Junior year, my friend met someone new at a football game and immediately noticed a spark. She said it felt like they had known each other for years. Within two weeks, they were practically sisters. She felt happier being with a friend she had just met for two weeks than being with a friend she'd known for seven years. Great friendships have no time limit or time requirements. The world is full of both negative and positive people. Your friends can influence you into becoming one or the other.

You should look for in a friend the same things you look for in a mentor: Someone who wants what's best for you and genuinely supports you. Anyone who does those things is already a pretty cool person. Start avoiding making friendships with toxic people who are very negative and want everybody to hate their lives just as much as they do. I am very fortunate enough to have some amazing friends, some of which I've known since 1st grade. What my friends and I all share are the common virtues of respect, support, and acceptance of one another. That's what a good friendship should be. Common interests like books, sports, movies, ideas are what make a certain "type" of friendship, but it's virtues like respect, trust, encouragement and affection that build a friendship in the first place. People like to find friends who are just like them. There's nothing wrong with that, except when you have bad habits like being lazy, moody, or complaining a lot. If you find friends who have the same bad habits that you have, you're only going to double and worsen those habits. If you know you have some of those bad habits like laziness, make friends with someone who works out every day, or gets up early, or is always motivated. If you're a shy person, make friends with a really outgoing person. Nothing can influence you more than the people you associate yourself with. Start getting rid of your toxic friends who contribute absolutely nothing to your life and start appreciating the great friends you have and make friends with people you know will inspire you!

Family (Degrading vs. Supporting)

Family is an interesting topic. Family is like that friend you can't get rid of, so you might as well treat it nicely. I'm a believer that children are only the products of their home-life. As children, all we do is imitate. We learn by what we see and hear. As we get older, during the grade school phase, we start making our own decisions based on what we've learned at home. High school is usually the time when kids start having their own ideas that could be different than their family. A couple of years into adulthood is when a person stays in one place, whether it's completely different from their home-life or exactly the same. I've seen it all. Throughout this journey of growing up, one might always bump heads with their family, or be completely supported. I have a family that's a mixture of both. I have friends who have family that are on extreme opposite sides of the spectrum. Let's examine those first and see how we can react to them.

Believe it or not, families can be just as toxic as friendships. Perhaps even more toxic since you have to live with them. Not everybody is made out to be a sibling, parent, cousin, aunt or uncle. Those are simply just titles. Words are only groups of sounds that humans add meaning to. The word "mother" could be the most beautiful thing to one person, while having no significant value to another. The point I'm trying to make is that not everybody has a great family. I know kids who get involved in after-school activities so they won't have to go home. A common thing I've observed within a lot of those kids is the lack of receiving support and affection. They get awkward when they receive a compliment, and almost cry when you show some support. I've seen it all. If you fall under this category, I suggest applying some concepts from previous chapters: *Understand, Do It Yourself* and *Treat Others Like You Want To Be Treated*.

I hear a lot of kids saying their family doesn't support them, which might sound ironic but sometimes makes sense. Your family only sees you as a direct replica of themselves. If you have a parent that's a doctor, they'll expect you to be completely sophisticated. If you have a parent who is not creative, they'll say all your ideas don't make sense. If you find yourself in a position where you think your family doesn't value your dreams and ambitions, ask yourself what type of people your parents and siblings are. Would they ever want to do what you want to do? Does their type of personality match up with your type of goals? If the answer is no, then the typical thing would be is that they won't support you. I love Theatre. My mom doesn't. My mom isn't a big supporter of my dreams, not because she doesn't love me, but because she doesn't understand Theatre since she was never exposed to it, much less tried it. If you have a person in your family who never had their dream come true, or didn't have a dream to begin with, they might be the exact stormy cloud that walks over every one of your ideas. What you have to do is not have negative feelings towards that person, much less take it personal. What you have to do is evaluate the person in your family who doesn't believe in you, ask yourself questions about them, realize that they're not the person to support you anyway, and move on to the next step.

As much as you should love yourself, you should also support yourself. You literally have to be your own motivation. I can't tell you how many times I've watched motivational YouTube videos and got myself hyped up. I listen to music, read books and watch TedTalks just to get some fuel to keep me going. It's not that hard. The friends we have can sometimes be a great help, but they're not with us all the time. This is another practice of self-dependency. You have to be able to motivate yourself to do the last three push-ups, do the last math problem, or read the last chapter. There will be moments when you feel like no one is on your side. That's when you have to talk to the perfect version of you inside of you and remind yourself that you're really only doing it for yourself. Love yourself, support yourself, even when no one else does it.

Lastly, just because no one might take you seriously in your household, doesn't mean you should be a jerk either. If you're not so fond of the people living in your house, the absolute least you can do is treat them with respect. Respect should always be the bare minimum. The universe reciprocates (Chapter 4). Even if you don't get immediate respect back at home, the universe will give back respect some way or another. You might have a neighbor or teacher that will genuinely care about you. Regardless of how the universe reciprocates, treat your family with respect. It could be as simple as saying "Hi" and "Bye" or maybe asking them if they need anything. What's the other alternative? Hating your family? Not wanting to be home? Why add more fuel to the fire? You have the power to control an atmosphere. The first atmosphere you can influence starts at home.

What if you don't relate to the last three paragraphs? What if you and your family have an awesome relationship? That's great! But there are some things that you should always keep in mind, even when you have all the support you can get. With having a supportive family, always remember three concepts of previous chapters: *Make Your Voice Count*, *Be Grateful*, and *Give Back*.

Some families have it all planned out when a little one is born. They know what they're going to name you, what you're going to get involved in, what TV show you're going to watch, what your favorite music will be and even what sport teams you'll be rooting for. It's a big shocker when their little munchkin grows up and starts having their own ideas. If you find yourself in high school and realize that your family is still planning out everything for you without really taking your opinion under consideration, it's time for you to speak up. Some families love their children to death and could give them the entire world except for what they actually want. Start advocating for yourself. If they love you so much, they should be able to accommodate you. It could be as simple as kindly rejecting their Olive Garden offer because all you really want is McDonald's (Or vice-versa). It could be situations more serious like admitting that you want to study computer science when your family wanted you to be a doctor. Speaking up for yourself to a family that loves you so much can fill you with a sense of guiltiness, but just know that if you don't communicate honestly with your family, they are more than likely to have your life planned out for you, whether you like it or not.

Maybe your family is not over-the-top. Maybe your family is right in the middle. They support you when you need it and they're not on your back if they don't have to. The common thing that happens here is that we end up taking them for granted. We end up focusing on other people who support us in a fan-girl type of way, or people who wish we fail miserably. By focusing on those two groups, we forget to acknowledge that we have exactly what we want right at home. We tend to go to our family only if need something like money or permission and then go back to our own lives. We forget to be grateful. This simple little glitch can be solved by just saying "Thank You." You shouldn't only say it when you receive something. You should say it at random moments so you can remind your family that you genuinely appreciate them. You can also do something better: *Give Back.*

Aside from taking our family for granted, sometimes we forget that they are also human beings who need to be cared for and appreciated. Sometimes a "Thank You" isn't the only thing they deserve. If you have a family that shows you affection, make sure you show that affection back. Ask your siblings and parents how they're doing. Ask if you can do anything for them and remind them that you're always there to help them. Surprise them with random acts of kindness. Get them their favorite food or their favorite scented candle. I know many kids who have everything they could ask for at home, but never show any gratitude and much less give back to their family. The sooner you can be grateful and try to match their kindness of giving, the happier your environment will be.

Whether your family degrades you or supports you, you need to remember that you have the power to control the atmosphere. The bare minimum of respect can get you through the tough times, and random acts of kindness can double the best of times. Family is that friend you can't get rid of, so you might as well make it worth-while.

Romantic Relationships (Possessive vs. Comfort)

As one gets older, all kinds of relationships develop, especially the romantic ones. You get to a point where other boys or girls no longer have cooties and start looking attractive. I had my first relationship back in 5th grade. It was those kind of relationships where the two of you are best friends, ask each other out, then don't talk to each other anymore. But at the time, it was a thrill. Relationships got more serious throughout the years, which included holding hands under the lunch room table, walking your partner home, talking on the phone, and dare I say it, kisses on the cheek. Sounds like your typical middle school love saga. Like I said, at the time, it was riveting. Once I got into high school, relationships were practically the same thing, except now with the extra expense of money. Even though the physical things were the same, the mentality was not. Here's the number one thing I knew was a fact about high school relationships: *Immature people make immature couples.* Makes sense right? It makes perfect sense if your only definition of immaturity is acting goofy and laughing at dirty jokes. That's not all that immaturity is. Aside from acting childish, immaturity is more about not acting appropriate towards a certain situation. For example, I had a friend who met her boyfriend through the mobile app, Snapchat. I don't even want to get started on how terrible of a start that was. My friend proceeded to tell me that they snapped back and forth until he made the move and asked her out. After that, they went on their first physical date. That, my friends, is immature. It's so easy to talk sweet and hide your intentions behind a phone screen. If you want to know everything about a person through text before you even go out on a date, you're more likely to have a terrible relationship. Stop using social media to find relationships. Every day I used to see someone on Facebook posting about being single like if their contract just ended and they were now a free agent looking for the best offer. I'm literally cringing as I type this. That's immaturity in terms of getting into a relationship. There's another form of immaturity that goes on once you're in one. It's the worst thing ever: *Possessiveness.*

You do not own your partner. Let me repeat. You do not own your significant other! Once again, that makes sense, right? It makes sense if your only form of possessiveness is with materialistic things. Let me lay out an example. I know a lot of people who get mad if their significant other is talking to someone they don't like, even if their partner has nothing to do with that other person. I know people who get mad if their significant other goes out with their friends without telling them. I know people who get mad if their partner is wearing something they don't like. I know people who get frustrated if their significant other is not available at the time to hang out because they're busy. If one gets mad over their partner making individual decisions, that's *possessiveness.* They don't love their significant other, the simply want to *control them.*

The reason why couples get so possessive and jealous is usually due to the lack of communication and trust. Nowadays it's easier than ever to stalk somebody online. Once a person sees anything suspicious in their partner's social media, they immediately jump to conclusions. They try to suspend their partner's ability to talk to someone else besides them. People then get caught up in their heads and get defensive when they're told a compliment thinking that a stranger is hitting on them and immediately bring up that they have a significant other. It's a cause and effect of pure nonsense. If all you do is act defensive towards humanity and try to control your partner's life and actions, you are bound to have an extremely unhealthy and stressful life and relationship. Recording Artist, Drake, said "Jealously is only love and hate at the same time." That just shows what type of relationships he's had, which don't sound very good. Jealousy, in terms of relationships, is nothing more but a lack of trust, which is a result of lack of communication and not really getting to know your partner. Let me show you how it's really done.

For this example, I will be selfish and share the story of how my girlfriend and I got together. It sounds straight out of a movie, but I promise it's real. My girlfriend and I had known each other throughout all four years of high school but only started talking 2nd Semester of Junior year. We were both involved in the Spring Musical and had both just come out of bad relationships. We shared with each other how our last relationship ended, laughed and developed pretty cool chemistry with each other. A week after the Musical ended, I felt like I needed someone to talk to. The last month of school seemed crazy and I just wanted someone to listen to my thoughts. She was the first person who came to mind. I suggested to her that every night we'd text each other a confidential reflection of the day we had just experienced. She was getting ready to go on a week's vacation but agreed to text me back and forth. Her reflections sounded really sophisticated and almost seemed like poetry. When she came back from her trip I asked her if we could go out to breakfast. We went to our local IHOP and talked for about three hours non-stop. We talked about everything. Our life-stories, life-lessons, triumphs, failures, passions, ideas and philosophies. Every now and then I kept thinking "Where have you been my whole life?", as if we didn't go to high school for four years together. After our date, I didn't get her Snapchat and immediately ask her out. I knew that would've been *immature*. All we did was kept going on dates. That's what we called them, *dates*. Some of you reading this might think "I thought dating was when someone becomes your significant other?" It is, but the reason it's called "dating" is because of the way my girlfriend and I got together. We just went on multiple dates until we knew everything we liked and disliked about one another, and in this case, the likes outweighed the dislikes. I never asked her to be my girlfriend. After a couple dates we started hugging, holding hands, and doing all the lovey-dovey stuff little by little. Months later she called me her boyfriend and I called her my girlfriend. It just *happened*. Naturally and beautifully. No Social media was involved, only face-to-face communication, and lots of dates that developed affection, appreciation and trust.

That's only the story of how we got together. It's how our relationship functions is what I'm really proud of. Our relationship is based on one key virtue: *Comfort*. We always agree that we want what's best for each other, not what benefits us. As Seniors in high school, college was a popular topic. We both had different dreams and were even thinking about different colleges. Right from the beginning we told each other that we would support each other 100% even if we weren't involved in the picture. I told her I didn't care if she went to school three hours away and had to break up with me. As long as she would be happy, I would be happy. That, my friends, is real love. That, my friends, is *maturity*.

A mature relationship is about supporting one another through the ups and downs. Nowadays if something goes wrong in a relationship, breaking up is the first thing a couple does. You will bump heads and disagree many times with your significant other, but it's how you're willing to understand and compromise that really shows the quality of the relationship. Provide comfort to you partner more than anything. As Dr. Gary Chapman said, people like to be loved in certain ways. Some people prefer being loved with physical affection, some with gifts, and others with just attention. Loving your partner the way you want to be loved, might not work for your partner at all. Provide comfort over everything. Comfort is an automatic in providing understanding and communication.

Everybody loves a shiny car, but people groan when it comes to cleaning it. Everybody loves being in love but think that one argument is the reason they're going to be forever alone. As you get older you discover the ugly truth that love is simply not strong enough. I agree with the idea that there's a difference between "loving" someone and "being in love" with someone. You can love someone or something but not deal with the obstacles or circumstances that comes with it or them. When you're in love with someone or something, you're passionate. Love is nothing but a positive feeling that leans towards affection, just as Happiness is a positive feeling that leans towards gratitude. You can love someone deeply, but break up with them as soon as there's a glitch you don't like. Being in love, you're willing to go down the sea and up the mountains to work things out because you truly care about the other person. It can be as easy as getting over who ate the other's leftovers, or something harder like forgiving each other for saying something you didn't mean. Communication, trust and comfort are virtues that can make and maintain a healthy relationship.

Relationships are easy to make, but hard to maintain. They can easily influence us and change the way we act. Depending on who we associate with, we can ultimately change for the better or for the worse. Pay attention to how your friends really contribute to your life. Start asking yourself what's the relationship between you and your family. Who supports you? Who doesn't? Ask yourself what type of relationship you have with your significant other? Is it possessive or comforting? If you're not in a relationship, what are the real things you're looking for in a person? Always remember that you have the power to control who you want and don't want in your life, if not that, the power to control the atmosphere and lighten your situation. Relationships can build you and break you. We've all been there, but now, hopefully, we can do a better job.

Chapter Challenge!

Make a list of friends who you know are always filled with positive vibes!

The only way to spread positivity is to recognize where it is. By acknowledging your best of friends, you will be more likely to hang out with them more.

List 3 ways you can better your atmosphere at home!

This can be as easy as saying "Hi" when you get home, or offering your family help around the house or with something they need. It could even be as simple as having a conversation and hearing what's on their mind.

Make a list of things you look for in a person!

Try your best to stay away from looks. If they look cute or pretty, so what? Looks are literally just looks. You can't talk or communicate with looks. Make a list of what you truly look for inside a person. Their values, interests, ideas, philosophies, anything!

List 3 ways you can better your relationship with your significant other!

How can you better the way in which you communicate? Are you loving each other the way you want to be loved or they way they want to be loved? When was the last time you went out on a date? Is all your communication through social media? The list is never-ending!

CHAPTER 12 : MINIMALISM

We always want what we don't have. Sometimes we even want what we don't need. Today, there are more than 2 billion square feet of storage units in the United States. Google it if you don't believe me. That means that people literally have so much stuff to the point their house, basements, attics, yards, or garages aren't enough to store everything. How much do you want? The answer might be a lot. How much do you need? You might stall until you realize you actually don't need much. A couple months ago I watched a documentary called "The Minimalists" on Netflix where two guys by the names of Joshua Millburn and Ryan Nicodemus talked about dedicating their life to minimalism. What fascinated me the most about the documentary was the cutting down on materialistic things. That's what I'm going to share in this chapter. Minimalism, in the way I interpret it, is about one important thing: *Being Happy With Less*. There's two ways you can practice that: *Material Goals* and *Life Goals*.

Material Goals

First let's talk about the value of things. For example, I used know this old lady who got a jacket for Christmas every year. She had ten jackets in her closet. Even with ten jackets, she only liked to wear two. She had two that were her favorite and refused to wear the other ones.

Minimalism will tell you to just get rid of the other eight jackets. Instead of having then and only liking two, you would only have two jackets that would automatically increase their value to you. Those two jackets would mean the world to you. The less you have of something, the more value it actually has. The more value it has, the more you're willing to care, appreciate and maintain it. If you have 20 chicken nuggets, you could care less if one falls on the ground. If you have only four chicken nuggets, you will chew each and every one till it runs out of flavor. We think that having so much of something is great, but really all it does is make it just another ordinary thing that you won't end up caring about if it disappears.

After watching the minimalism documentary, I went down to my basement room and decided to clean it out. I was in shock when I realized I had filled up two big trash bags with stuff I didn't need. My room was pretty small to begin with and pretty well organized. Even then, I found myself throwing away CD's, papers, expired art supplies, files and books I had never used since I put them away. Once I tied the final knot in the trash bags, I felt as if my spirit had lost ten pounds. The room felt so empty, but in a good way. I was left with only the real stuff I actually used on a daily basis, and it felt so relieving. I watched videos on YouTube of people doing the same thing and throwing away five times as many trash bags I did. When you're left with the things you absolutely need, you feel more at peace with yourself and find value in everything you have. I had a TV in my room that I didn't turn on for a year. I got rid of it and had a sense of relief. If you know you're not going to use it, just get rid of it. Unless your passion is fashion, you don't need a unique outfit for every day of the year. Limit yourself to enough clothes for just a month or a few weeks and see how much less you have to stress about what to wear the next day. Less truly is more; more value, more happiness, more comfort. So go get rid of the things you don't need!

Life Goals

Growing up, we were told that a huge mansion, fancy car, swimming pool and huge TV were the keys to happiness. Are they cool things to have? I guess. But what exactly do you do with them? What's the point of a big house if you're only in two rooms? What makes a fancy sports car different than a regular car? Why do you need a TV to cover your whole wall? Do you even like swimming? If you really think about it, and I mean really think about (unless your passion is fashion, cars or I guess big swimming pools) all of these things have absolutely no real purpose. You can be more happy (and save a lot more money) with a lot more simpler things. The Minimalists showed some of the happiest people on earth who travel the country with only a book bag and a sleeping bag, and others who live in their vans. I'm not saying that you should go to those extremes, but I'm just saying that being happy with very minimal is very possible. There's a famous rap song by Biggie Smalls that says "Mo' Money, Mo' Problems." But really, it's more stuff, more problems. The more you have, the more you might have to pay to maintain, fix and replace things you might not even need, like jewelry or antiques.

This chapter is not about saving money or spending less. Although those are some of the best perks, the real purpose of minimalism is to be happy with less. The less you have, the less you stress and the more you appreciate. There are millionaires in the world who live the minimalist lifestyle. Just because they have money doesn't mean they spend it on useless things. Minimalist people often tend to travel or go to more events. They value experiences rather than materials. They value usefulness over quantity and quality. They value happiness over unnecessary stress. Being a minimalist doesn't mean quitting your job, being homeless and trying to be happy with it. It simply means being happy with the only things you need and value. Does your CD collection make you happy? Keep it! Do you know you're not going to wear those 30 bracelets? Get rid of them! Minimalism limits are different for everybody. For me, I'd be okay with ten outfits, three pairs of shoes, a toothbrush, soap, shampoo, two towels, my phone, my laptop, a speaker, headphones, my keys, my wallet, a notebook, a book and my keyboard. That's only 27 items, and 13 of them are clothes-related. For some of you it might be a bit more, for others, you'll be surprised that you only need less than 27 items.

Minimalism is about an everyday practice of being happy with the bare essentials that you need. It might be hard at first, but the new emptiness will be a relief that you haven't felt in years. Trust me, I felt it too. So go out there and be happy with less. I promise you it'll make a big difference socially, financially and in this case, the best way, spiritually.

Chapter Challenge!

Go to your room and clean everything out!

Sort out everything you have. On one side of your room put the things you absolutely need and a couple outfits. On the other side put things that you don't need or haven't used in a long time. Go for about a week or two living with only your essentials and put everything else away where you won't be able to get to it. If you managed perfectly for a week or two, get all the other stuff you put away and trash it, sell it, donate it, whatever you want to do, just get rid of it. Feel the relief and weight off your shoulders and consider yourself a "Minimalist."

CHAPTER 13 : STAY HEALTHY

All of the chapters so far have dealt with external and internal concepts. They've been based on ideas, philosophies and even guides to actions. Now let's talk about how to actually be able to do those things. A car can help you escape, play music for you, pick up your friends, store things for you and most importantly, take you places. However, every car also needs good maintenance, like good oil, good breaks, staying clean, and having gas. Those maintenance things are just like your health. If you're not in good condition, you won't be able to practice any of the internal and external concepts you've learned so far. When people think of "staying healthy", they might just think of yoga and salads. Though they are part of it, there is so much more. I consider myself pretty healthy, and I don't do yoga or eat salads. Sounds interesting already, doesn't it? When you think about health, think about three things: *Physical Health, Mental Health* and *Spiritual Health*.

Physical Health

Physical health is crucial. Let's start with diet. Almost every "food diet" I see consists of getting rid of junk food completely and eating healthier alternatives. That might work for some people, but for people like me, it really didn't. I would practically starve myself with "healthy alternatives" during the week and overeat junk food on the weekend and go back to level zero. There are two keys to a comfortable diet: *Proportions* and *Balance*.

My mom always told me that it's not what you eat, it's how much you eat of it. A slice of pizza won't hurt you, but 18 might. One water bottle is great, but 20 water bottles might make you sick. It's about proportions. I used to spend $20 at McDonald's all by myself, practically getting everything on the menu. Once I started practicing proportions and thinking back to minimalism, I would only spend $8 to $10 and have a great meal. I wouldn't leave hungry or full, but satisfied. I didn't go home looking for more food, or rush to get to the bathroom. My tummy and wallet felt completely happy with my decision. Cutting down proportions might be harder to do with junk food than healthy food. That's okay, it's part of the process! No matter what you're eating, cut down your proportions to what you think will satisfy you, but not make you full. You're getting five tacos? Only get three. Getting four slices of pizza? Only get two. Are you getting your fourth refill of lemonade? Stay content with the three you already had. Stop eating until you have to unbutton your pants and take a nap on the table. Thanksgiving scares me sometimes by seeing how people overeat and regret it the same night or the next morning. If you cut down your proportions, you'll both be satisfied and comfortable. Start practicing that right away!

The next thing to think about with diet is *balance*. Every meal my mom would cook for my family would consists of the main food (like chicken, fish, pork), a side (like beans, rice, macaroni) and vegetables (lettuce, carrots, broccoli). Dessert would either be something sweet like ice cream or a small bowl of fruit. Our dinners had a variety of everything. Keeping a balance is so helpful because it gives your body all the nutrients it needs. Even if my family ordered pizza, my mom would still put vegetables on our plate to keep the balance. Are you going to eat a burger? Make yourself a little vegetable bowl too. Is your bowl of fruit really boring? Add some yogurt to it! Proportions well help your body feel good, balance will help your body do all the "behind the scenes" work in getting the nutrients you need and keeping you healthy.

The best way to practice these things is to go little by little. Don't cut your food proportions in half right away. Everybody eats differently. A wrestler and a football player, even while both being athletes, need to eat different sized proportions. Take it slow. If you're a polar eater, as in one meal is all junk and another all healthy, start mixing them together little by little. Your body truly is your temple. Take care of it the best way you can. What you eat is fine, as long as it's balanced and in good proportions.

Last but not least, exercise. I remember one day eating at Denny's, munching down a big waffle and looking up at their television screen that was showing a group of people working out and promoting a fitness program. I thought to myself "That looks really hard, but eating this waffle is really easy." We all have this wrong idea that working out is about wearing tight clothing, sweating excessively, running a marathon, and doing 1,000 sit-ups and push-ups. It's absolutely not. That's maybe when you're on level 100 and some type of athlete or performer. But what about for just staying healthy? How can you start? It's easy. First, start off by asking yourself how much do you work out anyway? Is it once a week? Once a day? Two times a month? Not at all? Everything in life takes practice. Working out is the best way to learn and experience that. Working out is not about making you look good (though that could be a result if you're consistent), it's about making you *feel* good. One might say "How can I feel good if I'm dying after every workout?" Working out comes with long-term benefits. There are no short-term benefits. Working out requires consistency in order to truly help you and make you feel good.

Do you want to start doing traditional workouts? Start measuring your limits. See how long or how far you can run before getting tired. See how many push-ups, sit-ups, and jumping jacks you can do before you run out of breath. See how much weight you can lift. See how far you can stretch. Take all those numbers and round it to the tenth number below it. Was your limit 24 push-ups? Round it to 20. Only ran for 17 minutes? Round it to ten. Anything under ten, you might want to keep as it is. Only did six pushups? Stick to six. Only ran four yards? Stick to four. After setting up your set points, start developing a rhythm. Do you only have time to work out once a week? Once a day? Three times a week? Whatever your schedule allows you to do, make sure it's consistent every week. If you work out once, wake up sore the next day, and wait till you're not sore anymore (which could be a long time) in order to work out again, you're only making your body weaker. Stay consistent with the schedule you decide to work out in and you'll start feeling better and stronger over time. Whenever you feel like your set points have become too easy, start doing more! Increase the numbers little by little. Depending on the person, the process of developing set points, being consistent and feeling better can take up to weeks or years. It's all a process, but it is one worth-while.

What if traditional workouts aren't your thing? What if you don't have time to workout at all? There are actually so many alternatives to working out. It's so easy. Start being intense with the movements you do every day. Is the place you're going to not that far? Walk there! Is the floor you're headed to not that high up? Take the stairs! Have a little kid you have to look over? Play tag with them at the park! Do you like a particular sport? Grab some friends and play with them. I can't tell you how many times I've had a good workout by just playing pick-up basketball games with friends. One time I decided not to be whack and went to my high school's Badminton camp just for the heck of it, and let's just say there wasn't a day where I left the gym with a dry shirt. There's so many little things we could do in our daily life that could help us break a little sweat. Here's my favorite alternative: *Dancing*. If you want a fun exercise, there's nothing I recommend more than dancing. Even if you "don't know" how to dance, try it anyway! Go on YouTube and look up Zumba Class videos, lock your room, and go crazy. If you do intense Zumba for at least 10-15 minutes a day, I promise you'll start feeling better in no time. Heck, you might even pick up some good dance moves. Dancing uses your whole body. At first, you might not have a single body part that won't be sore the next day, but with consistency, you'll be feeling more alive every day.

Physical health is so important in order for your body to function properly. Breathing heavy after climbing the stairs, walking, or running for a short time is not a good sign. Eating till you get full and uncomfortable is not a good sign. Start working out consistently, even if it's only for ten minutes, and work your way up to doing more to feel better and stronger. Start adding a balance to your daily meals and cut down your proportions to where you feel satisfied and comfortable. It might take some time, but it'll be worth it in the end. I promise.

Mental Health

Mental health is just as important as physical health. Some of the previous chapters are meant to directly influence your mental health. Concepts like optimism, self-love, self-forgiveness, gratitude and understanding are all to help keep your mental health well and consistent. If your mind was filled with the opposite of those positive concepts, there would be some big problems. In this section, I will talk about two things that are very important to remember in order to keep you sane: *Quitting Social Media* and *Getting Help*.

I know, I may have crossed the line with this one, but hear me out. Social media started out as a form to connect with people you know and with people you might want to know. As technology advanced throughout the years, social media grew and grew. It went from being a way to connect with your old and current friends, to having a list of a thousand "friends" who you don't even know. Sounds silly right? The problem with today's world is not the use of social media, it's the abuse of it. It went from being a way to share what you're up to in life to sharing everything you do in every minute of the day. Today it is so easy to influence and be influenced by social media. It's very easy for someone to pretend to be someone they're not and post something for fake attention or fake sympathy. People use their social media to inflict drama, make arguments, and troll other people with the protection of being behind a screen. Even friends that you know to be good people in person use their social media to share really whacky content. When I had Facebook, I only added people who I've had a face-to-face conversation with. Even then, I found my newsfeed filled with disgusting, dramatic and negative content. If you're the type that can scroll through your newsfeed for 15 minutes and only be exposed to negative content, you might not notice that it's affecting your mental health. Social media ends up eating you alive to the point where you're checking your phone periodically for no reason and focusing on everybody's life except your own. This sounds a bit extreme right? It's actually more common than you think. Social media has become the number one place where companies and organizations can market their product or idea. Some might have better intentions than others, but both types are out there and are only getting bigger. Everything on social media has become persuasive rather than factual. Everything might seem likes it's real, but is only fake content to make you believe a certain thing or be biased to a certain position. I see it consume kids my age more than ever. It's a really sad sight to see. What I recommend one to do, especially in high school, is to leave social media altogether. If you really want to keep in touch with a friend, get their phone number. If you want to hang out with somebody, call them and actually hang out, in person! Being in high school, some of the things you'll see on your news feed can be really toxic and influence your thoughts and actions. Stop focusing on what everybody else is doing or posting. Start realizing the value of actually talking to a person face-to-face, getting news from newspapers or websites, reading actual books, and going to actual places. Think of all the time you'll be saving yourself to actually be productive. I'm not saying leave technology altogether, I'm specifically targeting social media because that's where everyone is just giving their opinion or selling their product, which are things you really don't need in your life. So get away from it right now, and see what a difference it makes in your time management, your happiness, your productivity and overall, your mental health.

Even while knowing, being aware of, and practicing positive concepts, I want you remember an important thing. *It's okay to feel*. To *be* happy and positive is a practice. To *feel* happiness is spontaneous. To *be* happy is internal. To *feel* happy is external. If you see your favorite character die in a movie, you might feel sad. It's something external causing you to feel a spontaneous emotion. If you see a really cute puppy, you might feel happy. It's something external causing you to feel a spontaneous emotion. To be a happy and positive person takes a bit of consistent work and practice. This whole book is about practicing positivity and extending happiness. As much as you practice these concepts in your everyday life, I want you to know it's okay to *feel*. There are going to be moments when the rain makes you sad. There's going to be moments seeing a rainbow makes you happy. Not having your way can make you mad. Achieving your goals can make you shed tears of joy. As humans we are bound to have endless emotions throughout one day. Depending on our environment, sometimes we make the mistakes of bottling up our emotions or expressing them the wrong way. We bottle them up and end up looking like "Sadness" from the movie "Inside Out." We sometimes act spontaneously like the character "Anger", and we all know how spontaneous actions can lead to big regrets. It's okay to feel, but it's what we do with our feelings that determines the type of person that we are. That's where the practice of positive concepts come into play. As Recording Artist, Kanye West, said in one of his famous rants, "Feelings matter bro'." They certainly do. We treat having feelings as a sign of weakness. We see little boys and girls being raised to be really tough and bottle up their emotions. Bottling up emotions can have severe long-term consequences like stubbornness, bad attitudes, ungratefulness and a lack of empathy.

Feeling happy is a wonderful feeling we wish to last forever, but how does one express themselves when they're feeling sad, angry, frustrated or agitated? Sometimes little things like working out, going on a rant, or listening to some music can help you blow off some steam to get rid of a negative feeling. But what about when the feeling is constant? When you're not *feeling* negative, but rather *being* negative. Believe it or not, conditions like depression, anxiety and insanity are real things (another reason why you should leave social media). If you find yourself consistently being negative or being told that you're negative, consider getting some help, whether it's from your friends, family, mentor or a professional. You don't have to be ashamed about being sad or angry and wanting help. Sometimes that help could be as easy as talking to someone confidentially. Sometimes it can lead to bigger solutions like prescriptions or medication. It's okay to want what's best for you and go out there to obtain it. There are people who have professional jobs to help people with these types of problems. If you're constantly feeling a negative way, read this book and try some of its practices. If you feel that's it's taking you nowhere, consider getting some help. Don't be afraid to speak up for yourself. If you bottle your emotions, you'll end up suffering the long-term consequences and not end up being the person you want to be. Feelings matter. Those that say they don't, I can probably assume what type of person they are. I believe one should be ruthless when wanting to achieve their goals. I believe that one should never give up, and that they should be okay with a little pain that comes with the work. However, I also believe one should always acknowledge their feelings and work to better them by practicing concepts that are shared in this book. If negative feelings are constantly inevitable, just know that it's completely okay to get assistance. That's the best thing you can do for yourself and the people around you.

Spiritual Health

This is a section that I honestly can't really explain. It's also a feeling, but a different kind of feeling (I'm trying). Feelings are pretty spontaneous, but when you have a feeling with your spirit, it's a profound feeling beyond your physical existence. I'm not a big religious person, but I am a spiritual person. One, because everyone can see and hear without actually seeing and hearing (science probably has an answer to what exactly makes that happen but stay with me).

Two, everything can go perfectly fine and you might still feel a certain burden within yourself. I remember coming back from a Washington D.C. trip right after graduation and wanting to take a long break, even though everything was going great. I had just graduated high school, had a lot of fun in the last weeks of it, had just came from going to Washington D.C. to march in a parade, and had everything good to go for the summer and for college. Even while everything was perfectly fine, I needed a break. I felt tired. Not physically, not mentally, but spiritually. It's a feeling of wanting to be alone to take a big breath and absorb everything around you. This would be the perfect time to go to your escape, to bring you peace and back to level zero. Sometimes too much happiness can also be overwhelming. I've felt so happy before to the point I thought I was hallucinating and everything was just a dream. Spiritual health is about feeling grounded to the reality of the earth and the journey to your dreams. Being in nature is a great way to practice balancing your spiritual health. Taking deep breaths also works just as fine. Deep breaths can calm your heart beat, which can eventually change your feeling of being rushed to being really calm. Personally, I use the power of music. Going to your escape feeds directly to your spiritual health. The peace I get from listening to music is the peace my girlfriend gets when she's barefoot at a nature park. Being overwhelmed, whether because of stress or happiness, can knock the balance of your spiritual health. Go to your escape, take deep breaths or take a nature walk. The world is full of crazy things, ideas, events and people. No matter how peaceful you are as a person, the vibes coming from those negative things are hard to resist. But by keeping your spiritual health intact, it will be easier to avoid and remain positive.

Your health is important to maintain in order to function as a human and as the person you want to be. Keep your physical health intact by working out some sort of consistent way and by cutting down and balancing your food diet. Stay away from negative vibes on social media and don't be afraid to express your feelings if you're ever in the need of help. Take deep breaths and go to your escape when you feel a certain burden within you that you can't explain. Stay healthy, it's the only way you'll accomplish the task of staying alive and the art of living.

Chapter Challenge!

Make a log of the things you eat and how long you workout for a whole week!

After writing things down for a week, figure out what you can fix in your diet and what you can do to make your workout more consistent.

Try to spend a week without using any social media!

See what you do when you're not on your phone or on your computer. What will you do with that time? Try reading a book! Listen to an album! Actually hang out with your friends or talk on the phone! Anything!

Try going to a nature park and take deep breaths!

Being intact with nature can bring you a peace you never thought existed. Play some relaxing music too, it works!

CHAPTER 14 : DON'T GIVE UP

We hear it all the time. We hear it so much we actually don't know what it really means. "Don't give up." Three words wrapped in cheese but actually the hardest thing to do in your lifetime. Here's the hard truth: Everyone is motivated, putting in their 10,000 hours, ready to take over the world until the moment they fail. That moment of failure can literally traumatize you and kill your dream in an instant. People talk about persistence but only view it in the form of practice. They say you have to persist in practicing to get better. Persist when it hurts so you can get stronger. Persist to get out of your comfort zone and feel better. Although those are some parts of persistence, what it really comes down to is being able to get back up after failure and do it again. That's what persistence really is. How many failures can you go through before you give up? There are many people whose answer to that question has been "One." In order to really master the art of not giving up, you have to keep in mind three things: *The Process*, *The Failure* and *The Finish*.

The Process

Everything in life takes practice! Everything! You will not wake up one day being the happiest person on earth without PRACTICE. You will not wake up and be a better basketball player without PRACTICE. You will not land a role in your favorite play without PRACTICE. My favorite example to use is the iconic comedian, Kevin Hart. Kevin Hart took over the comedy world by storm a couple years ago and became a hit with his stand-up specials and movies. Although everything looked like it was going well for him, Kevin said that people were only seeing the tip of the iceberg. It took one year for Kevin to finally make it big, but before that, he said he was constantly rejected and going through failures for ten years. That's a really long time. It took Kevin a process of ten years in order to be the phenomenon he is today. Today we are fooled by TV and Social Media that one viral video is all you need to become famous. Sure one can go viral, maybe appear on a TV show, and burn out within four weeks. I think the bathroom breaks I need after a good burrito last longer than internet sensations. The advancement of technology is literally cutting our patience in half. Humans are so obsessed with having everything be fast. Fast Internet. Fast Phone. Fast Cars. Fast Food. Fast Service. No one has patience for anything. If one does not have patience for simple things, they're not going to have patience for the journey that awaits them when making a dream come true. Recognize that everything takes a process. Any great invention took thousands of trials before it came to exist. Artists work on years to make the perfect album. Olympians practice for four years so they can perform for ten seconds. Have patience, work hard and you'll be one step closer to your goal.

The Failure

One of the worst feelings a human can experience is trying their absolute best and not being good enough. I choked up as I was typing that sentence. The feeling can traumatize you and discourage you from trying again. Even though I've experienced the worst of those feelings, I'm still a believer in one thing: *True failure is when you give up*. Failing is inevitable. We do it twice as much as winning. It can be as small as being late for work or as dramatic as missing the game-winning shot. You will fail 10,000 times before you succeed once. The world that you are living in is designed for you to fail. Kids grow up thinking they can be whatever they want to be and get slapped in the face by reality and adulthood. I know, it sounds very harsh, but it's the absolute truth. You have to be willing to take failures in order to learn, get better and try again. It's part of the process! It's okay to fail! The true failure comes when you stop trying. When you give up, you admit that it was too hard for you. You admit that you didn't have the persistence to make your dream come true. You admit that you didn't really care about your dream to begin with. Life is not about rising, it's about learning how to get back up, again and again. Practice will make you better, persistence will get you farther.

The Finish

I'm also a believer in another thing: *Finish whatever you start*. If you're growing impatient while working on a project, remind yourself of a couple questions. Are you going to come this far for nothing? What's the alternative, letting the idea die? You're literally only going to do half of it? Finish what you start! Pushing through and finishing can help you create that art piece you've always wanted. It could write the exact paper you wanted to turn in for class. It could be those extra calories you wanted to burn. It could be that poem you wanted to finish. It could be that final move to get the special person to finally go on a date with you. Finish what you start, and you'll never know what may be on the other side. Lin Manuel Miranda, creator of the hit musical *Hamilton*, took seven years to write the play. Someone had asked him if there were any moments in which he wanted to give up. He said there was actually too many moments where he wanted to give up. It felt like it was taking forever. He, however, didn't want to write up to four years and let an idea die. He persisted through the demos, rough drafts, critics, and re-writing until he finally finished the product he wanted after seven years. The musical today is said to be one of the most revolutionary plays that has ever hit Broadway. Finish your goal and I promise it will be worth it.

You can literally search up "Rags To Riches" stories and find the biographies of all your favorite celebrities. Everybody wants to be successful, but nobody wants to do the work. Nobody wants to go through the failure and get back up. Trying and attempting is already half the process. Every time you get knocked down, you will rise again and come back stronger. How bad do you really want your dream to come true? You have to want it like if your life depended on it. Your happiness pretty much depends on your dreams. So fight for it like there's no tomorrow! I see it as one huge marathon. If 100 people all had the same goal, but everybody had to run 26 miles, the person who runs the complete 26 miles will achieve the goal. Many people will give up after 1 mile, 10 miles, even 20 miles. But if you push through the fatigue and the doubt, there will be no one behind you as you make it to the end. There's too many people in this world who failed once and gave up on their dream. Don't be that person, regardless of how bad the failure was. If you're truly passionate about your goals, you'll be 100% aware of the factors it takes to not give up and achieve your dreams. Start believing in yourself, do it yourself, practice and persist! I can't stress it enough. Stop paying attention to get-rich-quick-schemes or people who go viral. That stuff is all fake. Pay attention to process. Be patient with yourself. All great things take time, and your time to begin, is now.

Chapter Challenge!

Make a list of 3 things that have to be part of the process to achieve your goals!

What are things you know you have to do in order to get closer to your dream? Are there skills you have to develop? Courses you have to take? Workout plans you have to do? What has to be part of your process?

Make a list of 2 failures that have impacted your life and forgive yourself!

Sometimes we have to look back on our failures and realize they weren't that bad. By forgiving ourselves, we can take that chip off our shoulders and focus on our next attempt.

Make a list of 3 ideas you will want to execute and finish this time around!

We all have wonderful ideas that we never actually do. What are some things you're going to actually do this time? Are you finally going to clean your room? Bake those cookies? Write that book? Talk to that one old friend? Go out for a jog? Get out there, start it, and finish it!

CHAPTER 15 : BE A LEADER

People think that some are born leaders and others are born followers. That itself is a myth. Everyone and anyone has the potential to be a leader, it just comes with some life-dedicating qualities, which no one ever wants to do. Some of us are very quick to point the finger at someone to blame, take all the credit when something goes right, or look at someone else to solve a problem, all of which are opposite of what a leader does. Being a leader doesn't mean being the best. Just because you're the best at what you do, doesn't always mean that you will be the leader. Lionel Messi and Cristiano Ronaldo are the two best soccer players in the world. However, when it comes to a penalty series, Messi is the first one to kick and the Ronaldo is the last one to kick. One wants to start off by setting the example, and one wants to claim the victory in the end. Even though they're both the best at what they do, one of them is a better leader. When thinking about being a leader, keep in mind three things: *The Example*, *The Responsibility* and *The Encouragement*.

The Example

We all know that one person who tells you what to do without actually doing it themselves. It can be your uncle telling you to not drink alcohol as he opens a can of beer. It could be your dentist telling you to brush your teeth while they have the worst breath. Before a leader starts leading verbally, they must lead through action. In order to change the world, first you must change yourself. Leading by example can be very difficult because it requires action. Anyone can say what someone "should" do or "can" do, but not many people can actually do it. If you truly want to be a leader, start setting the example. If you find yourself in a situation where no one is trying to figure out a solution, be the first one to step up. If you're in the middle of an argument with other people, step in and settle a compromise. Has it been hours that your friends stay in one place because they can't agree on where to go? Step in and make a decision. Refer back to Chapter 8 and "Do It Yourself." Becoming a leader can develop by stepping up to stressful and confusing situations. A true leader not only steps up in situations, but simply lives the lifestyle.

Everybody wants to start a revolution, but nobody wants to dedicate their life to it. When you're a leader, you have to be a leader 24/7. You have to be willing to set an example in and outside the theater, in and outside the office, in and outside the classroom or in and outside the gym. Your group will not take you seriously if you act one way around them and another when you're not. Their trust in you weakens. They won't think you're legit when you're trying to lead. In high school, I was always filled with positive vibes, even on social media. When my school started sharing my Facebook posts and Tweets, I felt pressured to be perfect with every post because my school viewed me as a leader and as a person who always had something positive to say. That's the person I wanted to be, but I soon realized that if I really wanted to spread positivity, I had to do it in and outside of school in order to make a difference.

Don't be afraid to step up to the plate when you have to. Leadership is about action, but not only verbally. When I was a Junior in high school Theatre, our leaders at the time were great people, but not the best leaders. I had a chance to step up and lead but I knew I couldn't, because I was a Junior and it wasn't my time. Instead, I chose to lead by example. I did everything I was told, added my own individual twist, and worked hard to set an example for my cast mates. I didn't say anything or give any speeches, but yet the leaders and directors were quick to acknowledge me and use me as an example to the cast. If you find yourself in a position where you can't take charge because it's either not your position or not your time, the best thing to do is lead by example. It can be twice as powerful, trust me.

If you want to be respected as a leader, you have to step up to situations no one else wants to face and lead by example, whether it's in your everyday life to be taken seriously, or because it's your only choice. Breathe in, exhale, lead!

The Responsibility

Being a leader takes a word that a lot of adults don't like. It's called *responsibility*. As you get older, your responsibilities double. If you're a leader, they triple. The responsibility of a leader is making sure everyone in your group knows what they have to do, when they have to do it, and where they have to do it. It can be making sure everyone is on time for the field trip bus. It can be making sure everyone knows their lines. It can be making sure your teammate remembers the play from practice. It can be making sure every child has their seat belt on. Responsibility to a leader is a big check-list of to-do's and do-not's. Sometimes they can be easy like counting to make sure everyone is there. Other times it can be hard like organizing a huge party. Point is, there's a lot to do. A lot of people make the decision of becoming a leader and being a living example of it every day, but as soon as they get to day two, they realize how much they actually need to do and how tiring it is. Not only is it tiring, but sometimes it's non-rewarding, on purpose. Let me explain.

There's nothing more trashy than a leader who gets things done and glorifies themselves. All I can think about is "So? Isn't that your job?" A common mistake leaders tend to do is being harsh on their team or group when they mess up. They're quick to punish when something goes wrong. They also make the huge mistake of praising themselves when something goes right. By only acknowledging yourself, you discredit everyone around who helps make things possible. A true leader does the exact opposite. A true leader takes the blame when something malfunctions, regardless of what it is. Even if it really had nothing to do with them, they still take the blame. They take the blame to make sure their teammate or group member doesn't feel so bad and to remind everybody that it's a team and group effort. I've seen managers at restaurants go to customers after their employee spilled their drinks and say "I apologize on behalf of the restaurant." They didn't say "I'm sorry, that waitress/waiter is so clumsy." By taking ownership of the mistake, you get more respect from your group, team, customers, family, friends and audience. Take responsibility, even when it's not the prettiest situation. There's one more thing!

Aside from stepping up and taking responsibility, you have to remember one of the most important factors: *Encouragement*.

The Encouragement

A great responsibility that a leader must take on is the ability to encourage their team or group. In high school Theater, after every rehearsal, I'd tell as many as my cast members that they did a great job. After a while, they were telling other cast members the same thing. It would be about three minutes of positivity and reassurance after every rehearsal. Before we did a show I'd get them all in a circle, made them hold hands and would give a motivational speech. Before the last show of the year I hosted a little ceremony for the cast hours before call-time to acknowledge everybody who participated and made them certificates. I did everything I could to make sure my cast was always feeling good and motivated. A true leader is always making sure their team or group is feeling okay. Sometimes it takes a small side conversation, a hug, a high five or in special occasions, commending a member in front of the whole team or group. A leader must make sure that every single person knows that they are appreciated and they serve great value to the group or team. If something goes wrong, you take the blame. If something goes wonderful, you praise your team or group and leave no credit to yourself. If you *follow* those rules, your team or group will give you all the praises you never asked for. If you truly *believe* in these rules, you won't follow them because that's just what a good leader *does*, you'll follow them naturally because that's what a true leader *is*. You'll *want* to take the blame and back up your squad. You'll think you don't *deserve* any credit for your team or group's great time or performance. Being a leader is about being humble, responsible and consistently positive. It's also a practice, just like everything else in the world.

The world is full of followers, and not only on social media. One can easily be a follower of someone's directions, teachings, ideas, actions and opinions. Sometimes following can be great and/or terrible. But to be a true leader, whether it's for your high school play, sport team or friend's birthday party, you have to do keep in the mind the three amazing tasks a leader must keep up with are setting the example, taking on the responsibility and motivating their crew. Go be the leader you never thought you could be. Sometimes it can even mean shooting the first penalty kick.

Chapter Challenge!

Make a list of 3 constant situations you see where you could start taking action and begin to lead!

It can be as simple as being the first one to raise their hand in a class discussion. It can be as big as planning a party. Think of things you see consistently where nobody wants to be brave and step up to the plate!

Make a List 3 responsibilities you have to take up in order to lead in the field that you want to!

Now that you want to be a leader in three consistent things you see, what are some of the things you have to keep in mind in order to everything to function well? Consider this your check-list!

Make a list of 3 ways you can start doing to encourage your team or group!

This can be as simple as getting everybody little lollipops, preparing a motivational speech, or putting together a fun music playlist. What can keep your squad feeling good and motivated?

CHAPTER 16 : BE FREE

Everybody wants to be free, but nobody knows how. People think "Freedom" is a euphoric feeling that comes from passion or happiness. Though those are forms of freedom, true freedom is dependent on one thing: being *happy in your current state of existence in the universe*. Freedom isn't always about spontaneous moments of excitement. Freedom can be experienced in a simple conversation, reading a book, or the simplicity of making a decision to your liking. Freedom is about being content without everything around you and utilizing it to the best of your ability. Freedom is that feeling that comes with looking around you and thinking "This is great." As positive and easy as it sounds, it's actually quite hard to experience. There are so many external influences that prevent us from being free every day. Those influences change the way we feel and view ourselves internally and ends up creating a cycle of unfulfillment and a desire for temporary happiness. If order to truly live free, you have to remember three things: *Stop Living Externally*, *The Importance of the Present*, and *Happiness You Can Create*.

Stop Living Externally

The first step to freedom is to get rid of the world around you. I might've lost you already, but let me explain. Have you ever met someone who was really selfish and acted like it was their world and that you were just living in it? That's exactly what you have to think. Let me explain again before you close the book. Today we live with high insecurities. We think about what people think about us. We comment on what people do, eat and wear. We're quick to gossip and defend ourselves when we think we're being judged. We base our emotions off of circumstances around us and become slaves of society that go through the motions and rarely live for ourselves. We consume not for utility but for symbolism of status quo. We live our lives trying to outdo and impress other people and show off our success. We live externally, which can never allow you to truly be free. Living externally can only bring you temporary freedom because you'll only be reacting to the circumstances around you, rather than creating them yourself. This whole book is filled with chapters to help you start living internally. I have written them to remind you that you still have the power to be an individual, make your own decisions, and not follow the status quo of society when some of the things that come with it are completely useless and senseless.

To be free is to live internally and be conscience of your place in the world for your sake, not for anybody else. Stop caring so much about living up to society's expectations and start living for yourself. Start questioning everything you do with the question "Is this who I want to be? Does this serve purpose to my existence?" Sometimes the answers to those questions will motivate you to take a job, go to an audition, or pick a college. It'll lead you to not eat that 10th slice of pizza, not go to that party, or not drink alcohol. By living deliberately and purposely, you will feel free. When we think of freedom we think of roaming anywhere without any direction. That only gets you lost physically, mentally and spiritually. Freedom is living the way you want to live and feeling proud and excited about your decisions. I believe that every decision you make should have a purpose, even if the purpose is "having fun" or "not being whack." Those are valid and realistic reasons compared to "for no reason" answers, which are full of crap. Live internally, and the external world will never bother you, much less define you.

Importance of the Present

The euphoric, spontaneous feeling and practice of freedom is only possible to experience during one time period: *NOW*. Everybody spends time thinking about what happened in the past or anticipating what's coming in the future. People rarely acknowledge the gift of time itself, the present. Part of being free is engaging completely with the moments of the now. Time goes slow when you're thinking about the past or future. When you're fully focused on the present, time flies. I was fully engaged in every thought while writing this book and was surprised that two hours had passed after I had written one chapter. Keep in mind that I'm not a slow typer. When you're hooked on a good movie, book or conversation, time disappears and leaves you with complete appreciation towards what you're doing. This is obviously easier to do while working on your passion rather than a job you might hate, but we'll talk about that in a minute.

When you start acknowledging the present, you will begin to engage in it and start to feel free as time passes. Taking advantage of "now" will help you accomplish things you never thought you would. It will lead you to get into your "element" or your "zone." The harder it is for one to acknowledge the present, the harder is to feel free and happy. For example, let's say someone spends the day cherry-picking with their family, but the whole time they're thinking about hanging out with their friends at night. Later, when they're on their way to their friend's house, they're only thinking if their friends would want to get ice cream. When they're on their way to get ice cream, the person thinking of what their friends would want to do after. When their friends say they don't want to go out anywhere, the person is incredibly disappointed and considers it a bad day. The person literally spent so much time thinking about the next move that they weren't able to acknowledge that they actually hung out with their friends and had a good time. If the person would have engaged in the present moment with their friends, they would of had a sense of freedom and happiness, for they would've been content with everything around them and appreciated every minute of it. To truly be free, one must realize the importance of the present and be determined and disciplined to accomplish the key factor: *Creating Happiness*.

Happiness You Can Create

Once you stop thinking and living externally, you become aware of all the time you have on your hands, especially the time right in front of you. The last thing to remember, in order to live and be free, is to remember that you have an incredible superpower: *The ability to create your own happiness*. You'll be surprised of how many people actually don't know that. People depend on materials, people and experiences to be 100% responsible for their happiness. There's no doubt those things can bring you happiness, but there's a difference between waiting for them and initiating them. Initiating happiness can be as easy as cooking your own meal, starting a conversation or giving out hugs and compliments. You have the power of smiling for no reason, dancing with no music, and singing your heart out off key. These are the same people that we look at with a side eye and think "They're so weird." But really, those are the same people who aren't living externally and could care less about what we think of them. They're being happy and free in their own little world, welcoming anybody who wants to join and ignoring anyone who doesn't.

There's not many other ways to be absolutely content with your surroundings and be engaged with your present other than being in circumstances in which you have created. When you create your own happiness, freedom becomes that euphoric and spontaneous feeling that becomes more and more natural with the decisions you make. But what if you're in a position where you don't like what you do, but have to do it for a bigger goal? It can be working a crappy job to pay for college, rent, or maybe some courses you have to take to achieve your major. When you're in a naturally negative-feeling causing position, freedom and happiness becomes a practice, which also works! You have the power to change the atmosphere of your circumstance with your perception and actions. Some positions might be harder than others for sure. My thinking is that if it truly is miserable all together, just leave. It wouldn't be good for your health if you stayed. However, if your position is not that bad and you're just in need of motivation, think about ways you may better your circumstance. Is it just a matter of putting on a smile in the morning? Thinking about the money you're making? The goal you're going to achieve? Can you turn some tasks into games? Do you simply just need to stop looking at the clock and fully engage in the present? With enough discipline, any one of those ways can work.

Everybody who complains is unaware that they have the power to create their happiness. While everybody would complain about math homework (which I equally hated) I would find ways to make it interesting. I would pretend I was some sort of Spy trying to crack a code. In my regular life I would also listen to positive music and put a smile on my face while walking down the streets and hallways. I chose to be positive. I chose to forget about the external things and focus on the present. Whether the thing I was doing was in my control or not, I made sure to make the absolute best out of it, because doing anything else would be a disservice to my overall existence and to the perfect version of myself living inside me. The world is truly yours, everyone else is just living in it.

Chapter Challenge!

List 3 things you have to start ignoring in the external world that you know will make you more happier!

Things like this could be a certain person's opinion, silly stuff you see on social media, actions that other people do that don't affect anyone, anything that you can leave alone in order to take a chip off your shoulder!

List 5 things you can do the moment you hit boredom or when you find yourself thinking too much about the past or future!

I don't believe in boredom. I think there's always something to do! Engage in the present and read a book, make a necklace, call up your grandma, do your homework, or hang out with your friends. Do something, NOW!

List 4 ways in which you can start creating your own happiness!

Find ways you can make yourself happy! This can be as simple as starting your day off with a motivational quote, listening to your favorite music, or my personal favorite, putting on a simple smile everywhere you go!

Epilogue : What Comes Next

High school taught me many things, both in and outside the classroom (mostly outside). I realized that knowledge comes from experience, but wisdom comes from reflection. If we do not reflect on our lives to better ourselves or remind ourselves of the person we want to be, we will never progress. We will never be human. Humanity has advanced so much over our years of existence. Humanity has been responsible for the most beautiful and ugliest things in the world. We're both flourishing and destroying. But while we're focusing on consuming or inventing the next gadget, we forget how to be human altogether. We forget to love, appreciate and connect with one another. We divide ourselves with man-made borders, race, religion, age, sex and class. The same things that makes us beautiful and unique are the same things that are rejected by a blind society.

To be human is to be strong and vulnerable. To be human is to be concrete and fluid. To be human is to love. To be human is to make the best out of your existence. No one is human anymore. Society has dedicated itself to producing robots who work until they die. Robots that lose emotion, ambition and fail to have a passion. Robots who live for the weekend to feed on million-dollar industries that provide liquids and drugs for them to feel numb to the misery, or produce a short burst of temporary fake happiness. This world can eat you alive if you let it.

Believe it or not, there's actually life after high school. If you don't start taking your life seriously now, reality will slap you in the face later.

Taking life seriously doesn't mean going all out in your education and getting a full time job your Junior year. Though you could do that, it's not exactly healthy, unless you have a different circumstance. What I mean by taking life seriously is living life purposely and intentionally. It's about enjoying every moment of your existence, whether you're feeling a rush of freedom on a roller coaster, or crying in your room over a breakup.

When I first started dating my girlfriend, my favorite slogan to use would be "It's a beautiful day to be alive." My girlfriend always answered with "It's a beautiful day to die young." I thought that it was kind of vulgar and that she was only saying it to mock me. However, one day she explained it to me. She said "Imagine that. A day so beautiful, that if it was your last, you'd be okay with it." My life changed that day. At the end of time, we all die. Endings exist. But when you're on your death bed, your fancy car, big house and expensive jewelry won't be around you. What will be around will be the people you love. People who changed your life. People whose life you changed. People who added value and happiness to your life. The day the world ends is the same day our heart stops beating. That fact creates two types of people: One who doesn't do anything because there's no point in building something that's going to end, and the other who takes advantage of every single day because it could end any second. Life is truly a blank slate. You have no control of what you're born into, but have all the power to change it.

We live life not knowing of the amazing opportunities out there waiting for us. Opportunities that we can create for ourselves. Life is about learning and doing it yourself. Absolutely nothing in life is simply handed to you. Those who stand still with their hands out are the ones who are shocked when life hits them in the face. Those who wake up every morning and set out to make it a better day than before, are the ones enjoy the fruits of life. The fruits of life are not materialistic at all. The fruits of life consist of good health, having a passion, loving yourself, being happy, being grateful, being patient, and having relationships full of love and support. That's what truly makes life beautiful.

So if you're a little munchkin in high school, wake up and realize that your life begins now. Practice being the person you want to be every day. Don't let life control you. You control it. While everyone else complained about how high school was terrible, I could say I had the time of my life because I did it the way I wanted to. I took and created opportunities for myself and many others. You have all the power to do the same.

To end this book, I'll leave you with the famous words my Sensei gave to me back when I was a munchkin in Tae Kwon Do class. I had just finished receiving my first black belt. My sensei congratulated me and told me this: *The sky is yours. Take it.* I didn't know what he meant at the time, but it stuck in my head ever since. After 18 years of learning these concepts, I'm excited to see how they will apply in the big world of college. I'll perhaps write another book four years from now. Until then, I'll continue *scraping the sky*.

A Special Thank You To

Mi Mama, Mi Papa, My Hermano

My Abuelita Lili, My Abuelito Tony

La Familia Zepeda (A Todos)

Rose Mozier

Heidi Soria, Natalie Cross

Mariana Cabrera, Ruby Cabrera, Adrian Czaja

Luis Rivas, Vanessa Cortez, Clarissa Munoz, Alejandra Viurquez

Larry Tyriq Henderson III

Karen Garica, Michelle Morales, Audel Ochoa, Percy Garay

Derrick Washington, Jasmine Gallegos

Martha Hernandez, Erica Hernandez, Nicandro Hernandez Jr.

Jose Manuel Barrios

Kayla Sutton, Klaudia Gorgon, Prince Washington

David Kelly, Ms. Custodio, Jennifer Gazda

Meredith Schilsky, Marco Lopez, The Warehouse Project & Gallery

Jeanette Soebbing, Nicole Durkin, Megan Fitzgerald

Angelique Grady with a side of Gravy

Rocio Hernandez, Federico Garcia

Jon Leonard, Nick Barrios, Danny Herrera

Jennifer Krikava, Joyce Zywica

Bryan McCormick, Thomas Mamminga, Cara Prochaska, Mathew Malloy

Christopher Covino, Kevin O'Mara, William Toulious, Jill Kingsfield

Gary Feltman, James Rodriguez, Pam McDonald

Pablo Yanez, Chai Tulani, Coach Moose

Texas Roadhouse Staff (C-Side)

Kevin Coval, Jamila Woods, Nate Marshall

Young Chicago Authors, Louder Than A Bomb Poetry Festival